United States–African Relations

Society and Politics in Africa

Yakubu Saaka
General Editor

Vol. 9

PETER LANG
New York • Washington, D.C./Baltimore • Bern
Frankfurt am Main • Berlin • Brussels • Vienna • Oxford

United States–African Relations

The Reagan-Bush Era

Edited by
Abdul Karim Bangura

PETER LANG
New York • Washington, D.C./Baltimore • Bern
Frankfurt am Main • Berlin • Brussels • Vienna • Oxford

Library of Congress Cataloging-in-Publication Data

United States–African relations: the Reagan-Bush era /
[edited by] Abdul Karim Bangura.
p. cm. – (Society and politics in Africa; vol. 9)
Includes bibliographical references and index.
1. Africa–Foreign relations–United States. 2. United States–
Foreign relations–Africa. 3. Africa–Foreign relations–1960–. 4. United
States–Foreign relations–1981–1989. 5. United States–Foreign
relations–1989–1993. I. Bangura, Abdul Karim. II. Series.
DT38.7.U54   327.7306–dc21   98-40604
ISBN 0-8204-4192-9
ISSN 1083-3323

Die Deutsche Bibliothek-CIP-Einheitsaufnahme

United States–African relations: the Reagan-Bush era /
ed. by: Abdul Karim Bangura.
–New York; Washington, D.C./Baltimore; Bern;
Frankfurt am Main; Berlin; Brussels; Vienna; Oxford: Lang.
(Society and politics in Africa; Vol. 9)
ISBN 0-8204-4192-9

© 2001 Peter Lang Publishing, Inc., New York

All rights reserved.
Reprint or reproduction, even partially, in all forms such as microfilm,
xerography, microfiche, microcard, and offset strictly prohibited.

To future generations
of Africans and Americans

Contents

Acknowledgments ix

Introduction
Abdul Karim Bangura 1

Chapter 1
The United States' Role in African Regional Wars
Ngozi Caleb Kamalu 5

Chapter 2
United States Policy Towards South Africa
Mohamed Sulaiman Dumbuya 25

Chapter 3
American Lobby Groups and
the Shaping of United States Policies toward Africa
Chris M. Kimaru 43

Chapter 4
United States Economic Assistance to Africa
Abdul Karim Bangura 69

Chapter 5
War and Democracy in the Waning Days
of the Cold War: Spillover Effects in Africa
Walter W. Hill, Jr. 95

Bibliography 105

Index 113

List of Contributors 121

Acknowledgments

Sincere gratitude is extended to the many people who made this book possible. Especially, I thank my colleagues, Ngozi Caleb Kamalu, Mohamed Sulaiman Dumbuya, Chris M. Kimaru, and Walter W. Hill, Jr. who took time off their busy academic schedules to write the various chapters for this book. More importantly, gratitude is extended to the families of the contributors to this book who patiently gave encouragement and displayed considerable forbearance during our preoccupation with this work.

Abdul Karim Bangura
Washington, DC
July 1998

Introduction

Abdul Karim Bangura

This book entails a comprehensive examination of United States-African relations during the Reagan-Bush era: that is, from 1980 to 1992. It seeks to fill the gap in the literature on the subject. This gap is a manifestation of the following factors: (a) the faint focus on United States foreign policies toward Africa in all three branches of the American government—executive, legislative, and judiciary; (b) the halting voice for Africa or for American interests there in the non-government organizations—think tanks, religious organizations, labor groups, and lobbies. With the disintegration of the eastern bloc, American policy-makers shifted their greater attention to that part of the world. As the attention of these policy-makers shifted, so did that of academicians. Since government and foundation resources have not favored the study of Africa in American universities, research on United States-African relations remains stunted compared to other parts of the world.

The limited federal support for African research in the United States goes all the way back to the late 1950s. Since 1959, the United States Department of Education Title VI budget, the prime federal support for African area and language studies, has given only 10 percent of its total fellowship and program funds for Africa compared to 51 percent for Asia and the republics of the Commonwealth of Independent States (sometimes referred to as the Newly Independent States).

THE PLAN OF THIS BOOK

In the chapters that follow, a number of issues that helped to shape United States-African relations from 1980 to 1992 are examined. While the major focus of these chapters is on this relatively more contemporary period, the analyses cull out evidence from earlier periods to give the reader an appreciation for the historical settings of the issues investigated.

In chapter one, Ngozi Kamalu examines the role of the American government in Africa's regional wars. The author focuses on conflicts in the Horn and Southern Africa as frames of reference. In both of these regions, Kamalu finds that American involvements were driven primarily by the urge to contain the spread of Communism.

Chapter two is Mohamed Dumbuya's study of American foreign policy towards South Africa. In this chapter, the writer examines the roles of the Reagan and Bush Administrations in shaping United States relations with the Pretoria government. In order to set the stage for his analysis, Dumbuya provides the reader with a synopsis of United States foreign policy in general. His general finding is that the Bush Administration's policy towards South Africa was not clearly defined and articulated as Reagan's "constructive engagement."

Chris Kimaru looks at the role of American lobby groups in shaping United States foreign policies toward Africa in chapter three. The author begins by examining the role that lobbying plays in United States policy-making in general and the influence and growth of lobby groups. He then moves on to tie American interests in Africa to the various interest groups that lobby the government and try to influence American foreign policies toward Africa. Finally, Kimaru focuses on Washington lobby firms that have become quite popular to African governments which often want to cut through red tape and get their issues to American policy-makers quickly. He concludes that the demand by African governments for Washington lobbyists will continue to grow. Kimaru cautions that African countries know their needs well before engaging these lobbyists, lest they get short changed.

In chapter four, Abdul Karim Bangura investigates the nature of United States economic assistance to Sub-Sahara African countries. The writer begins by delineating the trend in the level of American economic aid to that continent. In order to understand the low priority accorded Africa compared to other geopolitical regions in terms of foreign assistance dollars in recent years, Bangura examines American political perspectives and traditions that shape the way Americans see African and other developing countries, the purposes of American foreign aid, how United States foreign aid policies toward Africa are shaped, and the

Reagan and Bush Administrations' foreign aid doctrine. The major proposition in this chapter is that American economic assistance was concentrated in areas where the United States was perceived to have strategic interests, not in the poorest and neediest regions.

The final chapter (five) encompasses Walter Hill's examination of how war and the drive for democracy in the waning days of the Cold War affected Africa. The author argues that the change in nuclear capabilities led to the United States and the Soviet Union's attempt to find other outlets for competition in a relatively safe and open arena, namely the African-Asian bloc of nations. A careful examination of the African cases leads Hill to suggest an alternate interpretation which centers more on issues of decolonization and development. He concludes that these two realities shaped the views of American actors at the time.

In sum, the chapters in this book are closed sets within which it is easier to guess how and why new insights emerged, and what was overlooked. Occasionally, they provide 'new' ideas and rediscoveries.

Chapter One
The United States' Role in African Regional Wars

Ngozi Caleb Kamalu

This chapter explores the nature and scope of American involvement in contemporary wars in Africa. Conflicts in two regions of the continent are examined. They are the Horn and Southern Africa. In the Horn, the Somali-Ethiopian conflict serves as a frame of reference; while in Southern Africa, the conflict over Southwest Africa (now Namibia) and the Mozambican civil war serve as units of analysis. On the whole, this chapter observes that African regional conflicts serve as test cases for Soviet-American Cold War rivalry. In both regions, it is found that American involvement was driven primarily by the urge to contain the spread of communism.

This ideological motivation was reflected in all American multilateral negotiation strategies adopted to resolve Africa's regional disputes. The strategies were manifested in the form of linkages in which the settlement of policy issues were linked with the foreign policy behaviors of the Soviet Union and its ally, Cuba, in those regions of Africa. Thus, the United States mounted economic, political, and military pressures on the left-leaning or pro-East regimes to discourage their total dependence on the Soviet Union. By so doing, the United States was able to contain and even neutralize the Soviet ideological threat, while at the same time protecting its own vital sources of raw materials and trade routes.

The disintegration of the Soviet Union as a state marked the end of the Cold War in which ideological rivalry and balance of power formed the bases of United States-Soviet relations. This ideological divide defined major regional conflicts in Africa (see Hill's discussion in chapter five). The resurgence of economic nationalism and political developments in Europe suggest that little attention will be paid to both economic and political problems in Africa. Already, some evidence of this can be seen in Africa's declining economic assistance from major world donors (see Bangura's discussion of the American case in chapter four of this book). However, the Organization of African Unity (OAU) will continue to play a dominant role in various dimensions of conflict resolution in Africa. The extent and configurations of Africa's regional disputes will be contingent on the role of the United States in a unipolar world and the way power relations and alignments among the Russian Republics are shaped.

THE HORN OF AFRICA

The Horn became a major source of regional conflict in Africa when a once-localized conflict had degenerated into an international power struggle. In this region, there is the perennial feud involving Somalia and Kenya. Also, there is the Somali-Ethiopian hostility over control of the Ogaden. The latter serves as the frame of reference in the analysis of American role in this African hot spot.

The rivalry and conflict between Kenya and Somalia has its roots in the political map drawn by the European powers under the provisions of the Berlin Conference of the winter of 1884-1885. This early period of the so called "Scramble for Africa" was marked by efforts by the colonial powers to balkanize the African continent into colonies or spheres of influence. It was a colonial design to undertake the continental partition as a strategy to check their mutual rivalries. Hence, it was no surprise that Spain colonized the northwestern tip of Africa covering the area we now call Western Sahara which is being claimed by Morocco. On the west coast of Africa, the British established control over Gambia, Ghana, Nigeria, and Sierra Leone. In contrast, the French exercised control over Senegal, Mali, Guinea, Gabon, Cote d'Ivoire, and Francophone Cameroon. In the southern part of Africa, the Portuguese imposed their hegemony over Mozambique and Angola.

In the Horn, the Emperor of Ethiopia, Menelik, had exploited European rivalry to extend the territorial boundaries of his empire to envelope or encircle portions of Somali-speaking peoples into the Ogaden. According to Gambari (1991:10), these Somali-speaking people of the Ogaden owe allegiance and emotional attachment to their kith and kin across the border in contemporary Ethiopia.

The separation of peoples united by language, ethnicity, religion, and culture has become the permanent legacy of European colonial policy in Africa. This permanent division has turned out to be the most important causal factor of conflict in post-independent inter-African political relations. Hence, it was not a surprise that on recognizing this fact of life in the African political reality, the Organization of African Unity, as was observed by Foltz, enunciated the strict adherence to "the principle of territorial integrity, which enshrines the legitimacy of the borders inherited from the colonial period, no matter how arbitrary they may be about geographic feature or human population" (1991:352).

The social and political implications of this African "Berlin Wall" or "Iron Curtain," as it affected the ethnic Somali-speaking group in the Ethiopian Ogaden region, was more evident after Somalia gained its independence following the amalgamation of the Italian and British Protectorates. Somalia set forth the policy of incorporating all its "lost" people into a "Greater Somalia." The spirit of Somali nationalism is at the root of this movement. With President Siad Barre at the helm of power in Somalia at the time, he encouraged ethnic Somalis inhabiting the Ogaden in Ethiopia to rise up against the national government of Ethiopia headed by Mengistu Haile Mariam who was committed to the total preservation of the territorial integrity and sovereignty of Ethiopia.

The depth of the ideological commitments of both leaders played a role in their international alignment in terms of military support. Mengistu was perceived as an avowed communist whose appeal was well known in Moscow as opposed to the Somali leader, who, even though an ally of the Soviet Union at the time, was very sympathetic to the conservative Arab countries of the Middle East, such as Egypt and Saudi Arabia, which were friends of the United States. The ideological bend of these two antagonistic nations provided a test-case in the enduring Cold War between the super powers—the United States and the Soviet Union.

Siad Barre's uncompromising stand and commitment to the unification and integration of the Somali-speaking comrades made him extend massive military and economic support to the Western Somalia Liberation Front (WSLF), an ethnic Somali insurgency group fighting for the liberation of the Ogaden from Ethiopian control. This support and encouragement of the Somali government, both before and during the reign of Siad Barre, had enabled this guerilla movement to sustain resistance throughout the decades of the 1960s and the 1970s. According to Gilkes (1975:215-216), the WSLF was primarily made up of ethnic Ogadenis as well as ethnic populations of the Oromo who were spread across geographical areas extending into Borana and Bale with the intention of integrating this patch of land with Somalia upon liberation. Other pieces of territory subject to Somali incorporation include Harare and Arussi.

By 1977, what were initially regarded as border skirmishes between Somali-based insurgents and Ethiopian forces had become full fledged war with the introduction of Somali regular forces fighting side by side with WSLF fighters against the Ethiopian national army. With the territorial integrity of Ethiopia under threat of joint Somali and WSLF invasion, Ethiopia had no choice but to invite its friends for help. Thus, as Keller (1991:106) notes, the Soviet Union responded to Ethiopian requests with massive sea and airlift of arms and material. The Soviet military supply, worth over $1 billion, was complimented with the continuous intervention of 11,000 Cuban troops and 1,000 Soviet military personnel. With the assistance of these forces, Ethiopia was able to beat back and contain the Somali threat.

With the introduction of Soviet advisers and soldiers from its client state, Cuba, the Soviet Union enjoyed strategic advantage in the Horn over the United States. The establishment of the massive presence with proxy forces gave Moscow unmatched presence. With the Soviet presence, the once virtual Cold War between the superpowers was rekindled. Not only did the Soviets register enormous presence on the ground, they also became the new caretakers of the once American-controlled strategic facilities, which included the Kagnew base outside Asmara which the Ethiopian government had leased to the United States in its years of good relationship in return for financial and military assistance estimated at about $159 million by 1970 (Nzongola-Ntalaja 1991:37).

The switching of sides by the Soviet Union left the Somali regime of Siad Barre and the American administration with no choice but to counteract Soviet Military build-up in Ethiopia. Thus, the United States and Somalia courted each other. In order for the United States to establish a foothold or beachhead in the region to challenge Soviet influence and help serve as the guarantor of Somali protection in the Horn, Somalia offered its port for American use in exchange for military supplies and logistic support. As Clude (1989:162) notes, this rapprochement gave the Americans access and control to the large naval, air, and communication complex at Berbera, which the Soviet Union had assisted Somalia in developing since 1962. With both superpowers establishing presence on land, sea, and air, the once localized war became internationalized and acquired an East-West significance.

A superpower presence in the Horn of Africa has a geopolitical significance. The area provides any power ready access to the hot spots of the Middle East and the Persian Gulf, in particular, a region which serves as the economic life-wire to the West in terms of access to vast oil wealth. The United States did not surrender the access and proximity this region provides to the unilateral control of hostile Soviet or its allied forces. American presence in this area not only safeguards the shipping lanes and access from the Mediterranean via the Red Sea, the Gulf of Aden to the Indian Ocean, but could serve as a staging ground to counter any threat to its friendly, conservative monarchical regimes in the Persian Gulf whenever they are threatened either internally or by external forces. These nations include Kuwait, Saudi Arabia, Egypt, and Jordan. The presence of the Superpowers ushered in a period of relative tranquility in Somali-Ethiopian relations as the once high-intensity conflict turned to a low-intensity conflict with no end in sight. A short-lived incursion by Ethiopia into Somalia in 1982, which was repulsed with American military assistance, brought out the significance of the position of the Organization of African Unity (OAU) as stipulated in Article III of its Charter: to adhere to the principle of non-interference in the internal affairs of other states and respect their sovereignty and territorial integrity (Woronoff 1970:643).

Having set the stage for the resolution of the border conflict between Ethiopia and Somalia, the OAU reached an agreement in 1988 in which the two warring states agreed, among other things, to cease hostility between them, withdraw support for insurgencies interfering in each other's internal affairs, and to mandate the appropriate OAU committee to iron out any standing disputes between them (*The Washington Times* April 3, 1988).

Despite the presence of the superpowers in the Horn, the situation did not get out of hand because of the restraint exhibited by the United States in compliance with the "Carter Doctrine." Under this Doctrine of "World Order," the President had opted for the reestablishment of American global influence and dominance in post-Vietnam war world with less reliance on the use of force, but with more focus on moral authority. Thus, he emphasized the promotion of world order in lieu of "communist containment" as the center piece of American foreign policy. In pursuit of this objective, Carter believed that in order to change the course and agenda of world politics and promote international peace and security, basic American attitudes toward the Soviet Union had to be changed. Consequently, he urged cooperation with the Soviet Union as a strategy of controlling regional tensions. But as Gambari observes, "the disagreements within the Carter Administration involving the national Security Advisor, Zbigniew Brzezinski, and the Secretary of State, Cyrus Vance, over appropriate United States policy towards Somalia weakened the force of United States intervention in the Horn conflict" (1991:12).

According to Clude (1989:159), the Soviet presence in the Horn of Africa compounded the Southern African equation by raising fears in the Reagan Administration that the Soviet Union could choke or cut the sea lanes in time of conflict to deny the West oil shipments from the Middle East which depended solely on the Cape route. Also, the West's main sources of strategic minerals could be deprived if the United States failed to reverse the Carter Doctrine and look at South Africa as a bulwark against Soviet expansionism in the region. Hence, the stage was set for a Soviet-American rivalry over the conflict in South West Africa.

THE CHALLENGE OF SOUTH WEST AFRICA (NAMIBIA)

With South West Africa posing an immense threat to American global economic and ideological interests, the Reagan Administration found the policy of "Constructive Engagement" palatable. This is an adapted policy of the Reagan Administration to the South African experience. The Reagan Administration had believed that the most feasible and practical approach to South African political reality was the avoidance of outright revolution. Hence, his administration opted for an American policy that strived to oppose any violent and radical approaches. It was also believed that through friendly relations, the Pretoria government could be persuaded to dismantle its Apartheid system. The Reagan policy, which relied on the doctrine of "quiet diplomacy" as the centerpiece of its foreign policy strategy towards South Africa, assumed that through "cooperative dependency between South Africa and the United States," Pretoria could not be pushed further into overt defiant behaviors which would be counter productive to United States foreign policy goals in the region. (For details of the policy of "Constructive Engagement," see Dumbuya's discussion in chapter two of this book.)

Consistent with the spirit of "constructive engagement," the United States flexed its muscle to protect South African interests, especially in the United Nations (over mandatory sanctions) by wielding its veto power in the Security Council. This attitude perhaps undergirds what Chester Crocker, the Architect of the policy and the United States Assistant Secretary of State for

African Affairs in the Reagan Administration, often referred to as the "Western Experience" in his description of South Africa's political history, development, and economic system.

The political intercourse with South Africa was promoted further by the United States in May 1981 with the invitation of South Africa's Foreign Minister, Roelof Pik Botha, to the White House. The high level meeting signified an improved state of relations between the two nations. Military cooperation between them was also enhanced with the routine exchange of military personnel and intelligence officers. There were high level discussions between officials of the South African Embassy in Washington and the officials of the American National Security Council and the Defense Department in 1979. There was also talk that the Reagan Administration was at the verge of resuming shipments of enriched uranium to South Africa. It should be noted that former President Jimmy Carter blocked such a move in 1975.

WESTERN FIVE (THE CONTACT GROUP)

Namibia, which was popularly known as South West Africa prior to its independence, had been under South African rule since 1920. Following the opinion of the International Court of Justice (ICJ) in July 1950, South West Africa became a territory under international mandate. It is required under international law that the administration of mandated territories be subject to international supervision (Bishop, Jr. 1956:1). It should be recalled that due to Germany's loss of World War I, Namibia, its colony, came under the mandate of the League of Nations and was entrusted to South Africa. After World War II, this trusteeship was reclaimed by the United Nations because South Africa refused to relinquish its control of Namibia.

Pressure for Namibian independence mounted in the wake of the passage of numerous United Nations resolutions calling for an end to South Africa's military occupation and exploitation followed by a United Nations supervised referendum to clear the way for Namibia's independence (Kuehnelt-Laddihn 1987:26). Thus, the South West Africa Peoples Organization (SWAPO) was declared the legal and authentic representative of the Namibian people. During the Carter Administration, a group of five Western states on a multilateral basis put forward a set of proposals aimed at winning South Africa's compliance to a peaceful settlement to the Namibian problem. It was calculated to break the impasse, since Pretoria had consistently refused to negotiate with SWAPO which was at the time widely regarded as the legitimate body representing the will and aspiration of the Namibian people. Members of the "Western Five" (Contact Group) comprised the United States, France, Canada, West Germany, and Britain.

South Africa had dragged its feet over the granting of self-determination to Namibia, partly because of geopolitical and strategic reasons. Walvis Bay, which is the only deep sea port in Namibia, has added great strategic significance to the region. The port was annexed by Britain in 1884 and later ceded to South Africa. Following the collapse of Portuguese colonialism in Angola, South Africa suffered a military setback after its bid to use National Union for Total Independence of Angola (UNITA), a proxy rebel army, to thwart the Popular Movement for the Liberation of Angola (MPLA) Government headed by Augustino Neto and supported by Cuba, failed. The Angola victory spelt a psychological victory for the Soviet Union which provided a significant amount of material for the resistance. With the independence of Zimbabwe in the 1980s, South Africa no longer enjoyed the "buffer" separating it from ANC liberation forces operating from Zambia.

The Western contact group became interested in settling the Namibian conflict primarily to serve its members' individual and collective interests (El-Chaise 1984:58). The history of the region had shown that if no peaceful transition took place, Western interests and influences would suffer in the end. The liberation experiences of Angola and Mozambique from the Portuguese, and later Zimbabwe from Britain, point to this reality. The group's choice was to help shape the course of political, economic, and social events in the region in a manner to guarantee and safeguard its vast investments.

These concerns and endeavors were guided by the basic principle that peaceful change short of outright revolution would better serve their interests, especially in the aspect of managing conflict to avoid the possibility of interrupting the free flow of commodities. The commodities in this case consist of coal, copper, nickel, platinum, and chromium, many of which are vital in the production of industrial and defense material.

Nonetheless, the Western Contact Group had exploited the Namibian conflict in a way to promote its global military, strategic, and ideological interests. Thus, the issue of Cuban troop presence in Angola was linked to South Africa's illegal occupation of Namibia. The demand of linking Cuban troop withdrawal from Angola to the disengagement of South African forces occupying Namibia contravened the United Nations conventions which respect the sovereignty of each nation and its right under international law to enter into treaties, friendships, and alliances with other countries and to honor the obligations appertaining in such relationships. They also indicated that Angola, under the "assertion of sovereignty rights," could seek the assistance of its friends and allies as was the case when it invited Cuban military intervention to help resist and counter South African military invasion in the 1970s.

THE BRAZZAVILLE PROTOCOL

On December 13, 1988, South Africa, Angola, and Cuba jointly signed a historic agreement which governed the phased withdrawal of Cuban troops stationed in Angola in return for the granting of independence to Namibia in 1989 (Lister and Varbaan 1989:18). The tripartite session between the governments of Angola, Cuba, and South Africa reached agreement on a set of essential principles to establish the basis for peace in South West Africa. Among these were the staged and total withdrawal of Cuban troops from the territory of Angola on the basis of an agreement between Angola and Cuba and the decision of both states to solicit the on-site verification of that withdrawal by the Security Council of the United Nations, and recognition of the mediating role of the government of the United States (*African Research Bulletin* 1988:37).

Namibia, a former German Colony, had been illegally occupied and administered by South Africa in violation of the United Nations Charter, mandate, and resolutions. The war of liberation had created a no-win situation in which all parties to the conflict showed weariness with no end in sight. Each party to the conflict was desperately anxious to find a way out, even if it involved saving face (Reiss 1988:31). Jonas Savimbi's forces controlled significant portions of Angola. His guerrillas staged hit-and-run attacks deep inside Angola. The situation was made easier by the fact that many MPLA and Cuban troops were tied up in support functions and services in Angola's cities and towns (Reed 1987:222).

The Cubans were under orders from Fidel Castro to minimize casualties and avoid high risk combat roles. They performed paramilitary and auxiliary services as garrison troops to defend cities, oil installations, and guard the Presidential Palace (Reed 1987:222-228).

The United States' mediated and brokered peace agreement marked a new era of relative peace in a Southern Africa, plagued by conflict and war sometimes caused and prolonged by superpower menace and rivalry. Although all parties to the Brazzaville Protocol hailed the agreement as a breakthrough on the Namibian issue, a major obstacle yet to be cleared was, according to Garcia (1988:29), the problem of integrating resistant UNITA forces into the Angolan national army. The Brazzaville Accord was criticized for not going far enough to address the root causes of the civil war. As Maceod and Wilde (1988:43) maintain, the agreement had the effect of evacuating foreign troops, while the central government of Angola fought it out with UNITA rebels. It should be recalled that the central government of Dos Santos refused steadfastly to negotiate with UNITA leader, Jonas Savimbi, who had demanded to share power with the ruling party in Angola.

While the Brazzaville Protocol was a psychological boost for the prospects of Namibian independence under United Nations Resolution 435, it was early to claim success because of South Africa's past record of cosmetic posturing which traditionally had regressed into "status quo ante." This is what accounts for the deeply rooted suspicion among Africans that South Africa could not be trusted to honor its obligations under the Brazzaville Protocol. Given its behavior at the time, SWAPO was alleged to have broken the spirit of the agreement when its forces crossed into Namibia instead of retiring to designated camps as provided by the agreement (Lister and Varbaan 1989:19).

A number of factors which shaped events leading to the Brazzaville Protocol are enumerated in the work of Valowitz and Rolfe (1987:76). One element was that Namibia had remained among a host of active players in the Namibian peace negotiations that also included South Africa, Angola, the United States, and the United Nations. Furthermore, two main actors, South Africa and Angola, whose efforts led to the Namibian breakthrough, had expressed concerns which were difficult to compromise. In the case of South Africa, control of Namibia provided it with a "buffer" that kept a variety of threatening influences at bay (Valowitz and Rolfe 1987:76). Also, the Angolan government was beset by UNITA insurgency that was expected to conform with the idea of sending home Cuban troops in compliance with South African preconditions for withdrawing from Namibia.

The chief mediator and architect of "Constructive Engagement," Chester Crocker, once described American and Soviet roles in the peace talks as "a case study of superpower efforts to support the resolution of regional conflicts" (1988:3-6). The Brazzaville Protocol served as a step forward to signing a formal treaty. The comprehensive treaty encompassed all peace principles discussed during the course of negotiation, including mechanisms for verification and implementation processes for Cuban troop withdrawal. According to Seligman (1988:230), the United States' brokered peace agreement had a tripartite foundation, among which were the withdrawal of Cuban troops from Angola, the removal of South African troops from Namibia, and the election of an independent government in Namibia under the auspices of the United Nations.

There was great optimism that SWAPO would emerge victorious in Namibia should free and fair elections be conducted. There was also no reason to suggest that any loss to SWAPO in Namibia could offset United States' successes in helping make Angola less dependent on the Soviet Union. Hence, the departure of South African forces was of little threat to the survival of Angola, given the fact that its main opposition, UNITA, was relatively weaker (Seligman 1988:230). In an article on the Reagan doctrine, Menges (1988:26-27) argues that the American support of the United Nations' plan for Namibia guaranteed the eventual takeover of power by SWAPO, a Soviet client committed to the imposition of pro-Soviet dictatorship like the one in Angola.

However, a dialectical view is posited by Knight (1987:30) who argues that East-West rivalry had stifled the Angolan progress towards resolving the conflict. The throwing of support to Angola and UNITA by the Soviet Union and the United States, respectively, created a no-win situation by either side. The geopolitical significance of Angola cast the former Portuguese colony into the midst of two great 20th Century opposing ideologies. The stake was heightened by the fact that any nation which successfully propped up a client state in the region was more likely to secure vital naval facilities within striking distance of sea lanes around the Cape of Good Hope. This prospect highlighted the strategic attributes of the Walvis Bay which is located in the western fringes of Angola with its corridor to the Atlantic. Thus, Angola became a testing ground for the "Reagan Doctrine," a policy of supporting insurgencies against the spread of Soviet influence (Knight 1987:30).

However, the prospect for a durable and lasting negotiated settlement on the South African question remained bright, even though the challenges confronting the United States and other parties had never been fully explored (Wolpe 1988:60-75). The New York treaty involved the United Nations Security Council by way of the provisions of its 1978 resolution calling for the unconditional South African withdrawal from Namibia. This demand revealed the level of elasticity of the treaty to warrant the transition from a regional framework to a global arrangement. The time table for Cuban withdrawal was planned in phases and agreed upon in Geneva, Switzerland in November 1988. It cleared the way for a United Nations supervised election for the independence of Namibia in the context of a significant reduction in the strength of Cuban troops in Angola. The aforementioned efforts culminated in the independence of Namibia on March 21, 1990.

THE CASE OF MOZAMBIQUE

Following the end of the Carter Administration in 1980, tensions between South Africa and its neighboring states mounted. Pretoria's destabilization campaign was heightened by its cross-border raids against the African National Congress (ANC) headquarters in Mozambique. At the same time, a South African-backed insurgency group, the Mozambican National Resistance Movement (RENAMO), was waging war against the Mozambican national government (Ajala 1984:113-115). Washington was worried that further escalation of the conflict would force Mozambique deeper into the Soviet orbit. It had also been a major United States concern to establish friendly relations with Mozambique. In doing so, it was thought by American officials that Soviet bloc involvement would be diminished.

It should be noted that after the independence of Zimbabwe in 1980, the Reagan Administration decided to establish its own niche in the foreign policy arena. There was enormous interest in the State Department that settlement of the South African problem would boost American influence and credibility throughout Africa. Conditions appeared ripe for a foreign policy success. In 1978, the United Nations Security Council adopted Resolution 435, which formed the centerpiece of the implementation plans for Namibian independence. All parties involved in the conflict accepted the plan in principle. The Botha Administration in South Africa made overtures to improve relations with the United States, especially given the sympathetic attitude of the United States towards the Apartheid regime. South Africa had been regarded by many in the United States administration as the last bastion of the West in its fight against communism. President Reagan had once said that the "United States would not turn its back on a country that stood by her in war"—a reference that South Africa fought on the American side during the

Second World War against Nazi Germany. This partly explains why Reagan opposed almost all forms of sanctions against South Africa.

The emergence of the Reagan presidency raised new hopes of restoring United States power and preeminence as a major actor in global affairs. In order to achieve this goal, Reagan grappled with the challenges posed by communist movements and ideologies world wide. In an attempt to impede the spread of communist ideology, Reagan opted to put political, military and economic pressures on Mozambique whose history, experience, and distaste for capitalism and embrace of socialist philosophy was no more a secret. Hence, the United States supported the Mozambican war of national liberation on the side of right-wing revolutionary movements. The Mozambican National Resistance Group (RENAMO) was supported against the central government. The group had received its military assistance and logistics from South Africa. The South African government under P.W. Botha had also extended diplomatic and economic aid to it. The bulk of the assistance was indirectly transferred by the United States through the South African government as part of an American global campaign, resistance, and network against communism.

By 1983, American destabilization pressures had begun to take their toll on Mozambique. The Reagan Administration reached an understanding following a high level dialogue between the United States and Mozambique. Shipment of defensive weapons and resumption of economic assistance were instituted. American multinationals were encouraged to invest in Mozambique in return for making internal economic reforms and a reduction in its anti-American stand. The agreement was designed to win Mozambique's support for American positions on the Namibian issue. Also, Mozambique was encouraged to enter into direct negotiations with South Africa over the presence of the ANC in its territory in return for South Africa to desist from its destabilization campaign against Mozambique.

The rapprochement paved the way for the signing of the Nkomati Accord in 1984. It was a bilateral, mutual, and nonaggression pact between South Africa and Mozambique. The spirit of the agreement was embodied in the provision not to allow their territories, territorial waters, or airspaces to be used as bases for military forces, organizations, or individuals planning to carry out acts of violence, terrorism, aggression, or destabilization against the territory, territorial integrity, and political independence of another (Tarka 1984:123). In compliance with the Nkomati Accord, South Africa proclaimed its willingness to halt assistance to RENAMO. Similarly, Mozambique agreed to close the office of the ANC in its capital, Maputo, which was being used as a staging ground and command post to mount attacks against Pretoria (Ajala 1984:114). Many intervening variables accounted for the drafting of the Nkomati Accord. One factor is the structural dependence of the Mozambican economy. Mozambique got its independence with an economy whose total infrastructure was tied to South Africa. The appendage nature of its economy symbolized the aftermath of the vestiges of Portuguese colonial policy in Africa (Tarka 1984:124). This reality is not limited to Mozambique. The economies of most African countries, including those of the Frontline States surrounding Pretoria, depend on South African outlets, especially its ports and railways which exported their diamond, copper, nickel, coal, and a number of other export commodities. Zimbabwe, Zambia, Malawi, Botswana, and Mozambique are cases in point (Tarka 1984:124-125).

Economic and political sabotage, triggered by a systematic destabilization campaign by South Africa, forced Mozambique to gravitate towards signing a bilateral accord with South Africa. Its economy had been stagnated following South Africa's support of RENAMO. RENAMO, through attacks on economic and political targets, succeeded in undermining the control of much of southern and central Mozambique. Its members kidnaped foreign experts, destroyed farms, killed farmers, and attacked and destroyed villages and towns. With explosives supplied by South Africa, RENAMO also destroyed power stations, roads and bridges, and disrupted electricity supplies. Also threatened was Mozambique's economic pillar and biggest foreign exchange earner, the Cabora Dam (Tarka 1984:124-125).

In January 1981, South African Commandos attacked buildings in Maputo which were suspected to be headquarters of the ANC. The raid cost untold economic damage and human losses and hardship. Further damage to the Mozambican economy was inflicted by the drought of the 1980s, which, according to United Nations estimates, affected more than five million people. The drought was described as the worst in the political history of Mozambique (Tarka 1984:125). The deteriorating state of the Mozambican economy, exacerbated by the intensification of South Africa's policy of intimidation and destabilization, eventually brought Mozambique to its knees. Hence, Mozambique was forced to the negotiating table with the Pretoria regime to reach agreements aimed at lessening tensions along its border with South Africa.

As Tarka (1984:125) observes, the Nkomati Accord had far-reaching political consequences and implications for Africa in general and the liberation movements in particular:

1. The agreement impeded efforts by the liberation movements to topple the Apartheid system, especially with the banning of military operations of the ANC from its staging areas in Mozambique and Zimbabwe.

2. The accord indicated that there was a limit to which Mozambique or any other African nation could unilaterally bear the brunt of liberation war.

3. It reminded the freedom fighters that their best chance for political independence from South Africa was more likely to be realized through intensification of internal struggle.

4. The Nkomati Accord became a tacit admittance on the part of South Africa that it had been involved in a destabilization campaign against the Frontline states.

5. The treaty indicated that Mozambique or any other member of the Southern African constellation of states was not ready to compromise its security, national interest and sovereignty under unbearable circumstances to the overall continental interest under the principle of Pan Africanism.

The United States' strategy of linkage in resolving the Mozambican problem registered some successes. In a report published by Maier (1989:A22), President Joaquim Chissano of Mozambique offered to open peace talks with RENAMO in exchange for its acceptance of a cease-fire and adherence to constitutional rule. Given the offer of an open dialogue with the rebel movements on ending the Mozambican civil war, the Mozambican national government took a quantum leap forward to peace by making a power-sharing offer to the resistance group. The significance of such a development is that this position had earlier been rebuffed by the government in Maputo. The closest the two parties had come was in relation to their amnesty law which was accepted by a significant portion of the rebel group. After the breakup of peace talks in October 1984, the Mozambican government rejected all contacts with RENAMO, which it characterized as a terrorist organization. The proposal condemned the use of violence for political settlement in the wake of a guaranteed right of full political participation.

An interesting aspect of the peace negotiation was the active participation of the church, the Mozambique Christian Council which is made up of 17 denominations. Their goal was to guide the country to the path of economic, social, and political stability, national integration and consolidation. In July 1989, the leader of the South African Ruling National Party and State President of South Africa, Frederick W. de Klerk, backed Mozambican President Joaquim Chissano's peace initiative by calling on RENAMO to lay down its arms and join the effort for a peaceful development in Mozambique (*The Washington Post* July 20, 1989:A25). Unfortunately, this move was followed by the cancellation of a planned meeting between a delegation of senior Mozambican church leaders and RENAMO leader Alfonso Dhlakama in Nairobi, Kenya. A week-long military offensive by a joint Mozambican and Zimbabwean forces had prevented Dhlakama from leaving RENAMO-controlled areas in the central province of Sofala to attend the meeting.

New progress was reported in the Mozambican front on reducing tensions in Southern Africa in the late 1980s. The development came with the decision by Mozambican Ruling Party, FRELIMO, to discard Marxist economic ideology and declare support for the adoption of a mixed economy while at the same time seeking a negotiated settlement with the rebel movement that has sustained over 10 years of insurgency. The decision was taken by the legislative body of FRELIMO (see, for example, Younghusband 1989:A7). The apparent ideological shift by Mozambique reflected a growing pragmatism in the one-party government of President Joaquim Chissano to attract increased Western economic support and investment. Although Mozambique had relied heavily on Soviet military assistance, it was the Western world that it desperately tried to lure into giving it much needed economic aid.

Thus, on the basis of the preceding motivations, the Mozambican government initiated substantive changes in language. The terms "Marxism" and "class struggle" were eliminated from its official documents. In 1987, it backed a tough economic recovery plan recommended by the International Monetary Fund (IMF). The plan steered Mozambique away from the Marxist notions of economic planning and centralized control (command economy) to a mixed or free market system.

The United States Congress had discussed plans to negotiate with

RENAMO and to encourage Apartheid reforms and talks between Pretoria and the ANC. Fruits of the Nkomati Accord were evident in November 1988 when South Africa provided logistic support and military training for Mozambican troops for their defense of the Cabora Bassa power installation which was under the threat of sabotage from RENAMO, a rebel group South Africa had historically supported militarily despite its denial of any official assistance. In order to assure continuity of the new political and economic relations forged, de Klerk visited Maputo to reassert his commitment to the new spirit of the accord with President Chissano. The South African government followed with a pledge to promote economic and political development activities between Mozambique and South Africa. The focus of developmental activities included the restoration of power flow from the Cabora Dam to South Africa; the promotion of tourism, fishing, mining, geological survey, trade and industry; the improvement of the Maputo Dam; cooperation in joint housing and agricultural programs; upgrading and dredging of Maputo Port to handle ocean-going vessels; and settlement of disputes over migrant labor by relaxing restrictions on Mozambican workers in South African mines (Strobel 1990:A10).

In January 1990, the Bush Administration informed the United States Congress that it no longer considered Mozambique a "Marxist-Leninist State." The Bush position was based on the premise that Mozambique no longer qualified as a communist state with a centrally-planned and controlled economy or militarily dependent on the Soviet Union (Strobel 1990:A10). The policy implication of this classification is that American transnational corporations entering into commercial agreements with Mozambique would be eligible for trade credits and insurance for commercial contracts from the United States Export-Import Bank. Hence, Mozambique qualified to buy $250 million worth of American-made jetliners for its national airline, LAM. With this transaction, the once strained relation between the United States and Mozambique was normalized.

Conclusion

American involvement in the Horn of Africa in the 1970s brought to light its Cold War relations with its arch rival, the Soviet Union. When the Somali-Ethiopian clashes over the Ogaden threatened Ethiopian sovereignty, it invited the help of its socialist friends. Soviet and Cuban presence grew in

Ethiopia and their control of the Kagnew base outside Asmara ignited an American response on the side of Somalia. Thus, the United States was able to exercise control over Somalia's naval, air, and communications complex at Berbera. The American presence safeguarded its shipping lanes and access from the Mediterranean Sea via the Red Sea to the Gulf of Aden and the Indian Ocean. Also, it provided the United States with a platform from which to launch counter attacks whenever the regimes of its friends in the Persian Gulf were threatened.

The United States, under the Reagan Administration, initiated the policy of "Constructive Engagement" as a way of maintaining American commercial and political interests with South Africa, while the process of negotiating the South African Internal Settlement continued. Consequently, the United States, working under the auspices of the Contact Group in order to safeguard Western commercial and strategic interests, made the withdrawal of Cuban troops from Angola contingent on the disengagement of South African forces occupying Namibia. The underlying ideological objective of containing the spread of communism in the entire Southern African region through the neutralization of Cuban influence and presence formed the basis of the Brazzaville Protocol. It was a regional agreement signed in December 1988 by Angola, South Africa, and Cuba which governed the phased withdrawal of Cuban troops stationed in Angola in return for the granting of independence to Namibia.

Concern over Soviet influence in Mozambique and the communist bloc support of the Mozambican national government fighting against South African-supported RENAMO led the United States to encourage a resumption of economic and military support to RENAMO through South Africa. The renunciation of this support was contingent on Mozambique's change of behavior towards South Africa, RENAMO, and the United States. Mozambique opted to cooperate with United States initiatives to prohibit the ANC from operating in South Africa from bases in Mozambique. This goal was also a fundamental element of the Nkomati Accord. The American strategy was designed to bring about a peaceful settlement of the conflict between South Africa and Mozambique in order to preserve the free flow of strategic mineral supplies to the West.

The dismemberment of the Soviet Union in 1991 and the emergence of Confederate Russian Republics (Association of Independent States) marked a new chapter in world affairs. Conflicts in Africa will no longer be defined or approached on East-West ideological basis, which was the manifestation of power relations in a bipolar world. With the Cold War over, much of the world, including Africa, now gravitates toward capitalism. This means that economics will define the basis of power relations in the post-Cold War era. The stature of the United Nations in the aftermath of the Gulf War has grown with those of regional organizations like the Organization of African Unity (OAU). Thus, the OAU will in the future play a more significant role in the resolution of regional conflicts in Africa.

The decline of the foreign assistance of major donors like the United States and Britain, coupled with Germany's challenges to integrate economically Eastern Germany, hamper Africa's prospects to receive increased development assistance in the future. Hence, events in Africa are bound to be relegated to the back of global economic and political agendas. However, the emergence of the United States as the single major actor in a unipolar world undoubtedly encourages new American initiatives in resolving problems confronting Africa. Signs of increased American involvement in African problems have been shown regarding famine in Somalia in late 1992 and early 1993, and also in its peace-keeping mission which was terminated in 1995. Other American assistance efforts have been demonstrated in the supervision of multi-party elections in South Africa in 1994; supervision of Eritrean referendum for independence from Ethiopia and military support for humanitarian relief operations in Rwanda since 1994.

Chapter Two
United States Policy Towards South Africa

Mohamed Sulaiman Dumbuya

INTRODUCTION

The purpose of this chapter is to examine United States foreign policy towards South Africa during the Reagan and Bush Administrations (1980-1992). It seeks to test the hypothesis that the "Communist Threat," rather than South Africa's predicament of Apartheid, was the paramount rationale for American foreign policy towards South Africa in the period under review. In meeting this objective, the chapter is divided into four sections and a conclusion. The chapter also presents a brief historical review of United States foreign policy in general. Additionally, it examines how President Bush's foreign policy towards South Africa differs from that of Reagan.

A HISTORICAL SYNOPSIS OF UNITED STATES FOREIGN POLICY

The foreign policy of a country is a line of action that its government adopts to promote its "national interests" in the international arena. National interests are the goals and objectives that a country seeks to accomplish. These interests reflect the wants and expectations of the civil society on the one hand, and the aims, wishes, and ambitions of its leaders on the other. Thus, foreign policy represents both the execution of a "national interest" and the endeavor to accomplish a country's expectations. A foreign policy is usually specific rather than general. More often than not, it exists for only a short period of time (Briggs 1968:6). Nevertheless, a country's foreign policy is often based on certain principles, ideas, and ideals that are regarded as an integral part of that country's historical experience(s).

The conclusion of World War II witnessed the emergence of the United States as a preponderant power in the international system. It came out of the war with not only a strong and stable economy, but also an enormous military capability and an enviable democratic system of government. It gradually became the leader of the so-called "Free World" (see Hill's discussion in chapter five of this book for more on this).

The Soviet Union, a country that had fought with the allied forces (including the United States) during World War II, became an adversary of the "Free World" after the war. This was mainly because it espoused an ideology or system of government (communism) that was diametrically opposed to the United States and the "Free World's" system of democracy. Communism, hence, became a cankerworm in the international system that the United States and the "Free World" sought to eliminate. The United States was also bent on containing the Soviet Union's "aggression."

Thus, after World War II, America's foreign policy was largely geared towards the spread of its democratic principles in the world. It was also oriented towards the perpetuation of its economic system of capitalism. More importantly, it was directed at eliminating communism and communist activities worldwide—championed by the Soviet Union for the most part. To be sure, most of United States post-World War II policies outside its border were largely determined by the part America played in thwarting the expansion of the communist way of life.

In the case of South Africa, as we shall see, United States foreign policy towards that country was not necessarily in response to the issue of Apartheid. But as with any other African States, United States foreign policy was, for the most part, based on the part South Africa played in countering and/or deterring the "Communist Threat." Certainly, South Africa's possesses four strategic minerals, chromium, manganese, vanadium, and platinum, vital to Western countries (refer to Bangura's discussion of the subject in chapter four of this book). It also occupied a strategic position in the now obsolete "East-West confrontation." These considerations, rather than Apartheid, dictated United States foreign policy to South Africa.

The history of United States foreign policy may be divided into two broad eras. The first runs from the achievement of republic status in 1776 until World War II, and the second from the end of World War II to the present. The first era may be regarded as a trying period in American history when it was seriously engaged in consolidating its territorial acquisitions. The United States also pursued economic and political developments which prepared it for its leadership role in international affairs after Second World War. This period was characterized not only by military expansion and purchase of territories, but also by a debate as to whether the United States should be actively involved (internationalism) or abstain (isolationism) from international affairs.

The United States did in fact execute both. The long tradition of America's isolation and withdrawal from the international system was articulated by its first president, George Washington, when he cautioned the United States to "steer clear of permanent alliances with any portion of the foreign globe" (Kegley and Wittkopf 1979:30). But it was then Secretary of State John Quincy Adams who explained why the United States should not be concerned with the affairs of others and how isolationism could be practiced, when he noted that:

> Whenever the standard of freedom and independence has been or shall be unfurled, there will her (America's) heart, her benediction, and her prayers be. But she goes not abroad in search of monsters to destroy. She is the well-wisher to the freedom and independence of all. She is the champion and vindicator of her own. She will recommend the general cause by the countenance of her voice, and by the benignant sympathy of her example...(otherwise) she might become the dictatress of the World. She would no longer be the ruler of her own spirit (Kegley and Wittkopf 1979:30-31).

Under the isolationist tradition, therefore, the United States was not to assume responsibility and leadership for activities in the world, even for what it claimed to represent, freedom. Its role in the world at that time was to be one of example, moderation, and rejection of aggressive and activist policies which would have been contrary to the cherished ideals of the Founding Fathers.

The United States also engaged in internationalism or globalism. It expanded its territory, power and influence by playing the game of international politics just like most large nations in history did. The diplomatic history of the United States is replete with many instances of its willingness and, in fact, engagement in expansionist endeavors. The acquisition of Florida, Puerto Rico, and Guam, and its activities in Latin America under the guise of the Monroe Doctrine are cases in point. Kegley and Wittkopf, for example, have argued that "Manifest Destiny" was little more than a crude euphemism for, and realization of, a policy of expulsion and extermination against what was, in contemporary terminology, a collection of "nonstate nations" (1979:31). In any case, the goals of United

States foreign policy within this first period were the export of its "democratic ideas" and the acquisition and consolidation of territories.

The period after World War II saw the United States emerging as a superpower or preponderant power with a new sense of responsibility. The debate over whether or not to intervene in the game of international politics was finally put to rest. The isolationist tradition was abandoned as subsequent events and circumstances of post-World War II rendered it obsolete. American leaders were henceforth charged with the responsibility of shaping the World into a form conducive to its security and interests.

President Truman was the one who set the tone for America's post-World War II policy in the so-called Truman Doctrine when he asserted the following:

> The Free peoples of the World look to us for support in maintaining their freedoms. If we falter in our leadership, we may endanger the peace of the world—and we shall surely endanger the welfare of our nation (Kegley and Wittkopf 1979:33).

The United States took up this global responsibility with a sense of religious mission. It stood for and became the custodian of freedom, justice, equality, and morality on the international arena. The United States was willing and ready to act abroad "for the good of others" to make the world "safe for democracy."

To be sure, United States leadership after World War II made the country active and constantly involved in nearly every sphere of international relations. Oftentimes, it was even involved in frenetic activities. For instance, it was actively involved in rebuilding Western Europe through the Marshall Plan[1]. Through the Truman Plan[2], the United States was able to "save" Greece and Turkey from going Communist like Bulgaria and Rumania. The United States established the North Atlantic Treaty Organization (NATO) to provide security for its European allies, which gave them confidence to reestablish political stability and, in turn, enhanced economic growth and development in Europe. The United States was also involved in the Korean and Vietnam wars[3]. It spent billions of dollars in aid programs in an effort to promote and stabilize international trade. America was also involved in an arms race with the Soviet Union[4].

Invariably, the aforementioned activities may be seen as attempts to uphold, safeguard, defend and promote America's and the "Free World's" democratic ideals. Nevertheless, they were geared purposefully toward the fulfillment of America's most crucial goal of containing Soviet and/or communist expansion.

The presumed challenge of international communism became a defining attribute of post-war American foreign policy. In fact, this fear played a major role in shaping the way the United States perceived the world. Although the Soviet Union fought on the side of the allied powers during World War II, it developed an ideological stance that was not in tune with that of the winning allied powers. Theirs' (Soviets) was communism. The United States, being the leader of free world ideals and principles, saw communism as a structured, doctrinaire belief system that was diametrically opposed to the "Western" vis-a-vis "American-way-of-life." Hence, the Soviet system was to be eliminated. Combating this threatening, adversarial ideology became almost an obsession to a point where some have argued that American foreign policy might have and, in fact, had become itself ideological (Parenti 1969). Anti-communism came to define whatever goals America pursued abroad.

Several reasons may be advanced for the United States' fear and apparent hatred of communism. First, there was the assumption that communism was an expansionist, crusading, and enduring ideology intent on converting the entire world to its beliefs. Secondly, there was the belief that communism was totalitarian and anti-democratic. Thus, it was seen as a real threat to freedom, liberty, and justice throughout the world. As President Dwight D. Eisenhower succinctly put it: "We face a hostile ideology—global in scope, atheistic in character, ruthless in purpose, and insidious in method" (cited in Kegley and Wittkopf 1979:38).

United States policy makers designed the policy of containment to block or, at best, eliminate communism wherever and whenever it raised its head on the international scene. The policy itself was based on an argument presented by George Kennan in an article published in *Foreign Policy* in 1947 under the pseudonym "X." In this piece, Kennan argued that Soviet leaders were insecure about their political ability to maintain power both within the Soviet Union and abroad. This insecurity, he continued, might lead to an activist and, perhaps, hostile Soviet foreign policy. In response to this position, Kennan advanced a view which became popular and was adopted as an official policy. He held that "In these circumstances, it is clear that the main element of any United States policy toward the Soviet Union must be that of a long-term, patient but firm and vigilant containment of Russian expansive tendencies" (1947:575).

Although Kennan was reportedly surprised, alarmed and angered by the way his statement was misinterpreted and eventually distorted, his view became the cornerstone and cardinal principle of United States foreign policy. Indeed, containment became the single foreign policy of the United States, and embraced everything else, even domestic politics. Containment was invoked by the United States in practically every continent. And it made the United States support and befriend the most unpopular leaders and undemocratic (reactionary) systems in the world: Mobutu Sese Seko (Zaire), Pinochet (Chile), Chaiang Kai-Shek (Taiwan), Batista (Cuba) and, of course, all the leaders of South Africa before Nelson Mandela. In essence, thwarting communist expansion rather than guiding, expanding, and defending the ideals of democracy became the single most important goal of American foreign policy.

UNITED STATES FOREIGN POLICY TOWARDS SOUTH AFRICA: "CONSTRUCTIVE ENGAGEMENT"?

United States foreign policy towards South Africa in the decade of the 1980s was a continuation of the policy of "Containment," first adopted by Harry Truman. In other words, United States foreign policy towards South Africa in the 1980s was not a direct response to the objective condition in South Africa, the Apartheid system, but a means of preempting or preventing South Africa and the region from falling under the influence and control of the former Soviet Union and communism.

South Africa did occupy a strategic position within the framework of the now obsolete East-West confrontation. This made it necessary for the United States to have her (South Africa) within its "sphere of influence." First of all, consider the Cape route. Oil tankers from the Persian Gulf and a great variety of merchant shipping lines use this route almost everyday on their way to North America and Europe. It is believed that without access to South Africa's ship repair and refueling facilities, Western commerce could not move quite freely. Arguments have also been put forward that without access to the naval base at Simonstown in times of war, there is the possibility that the United States Navy may not be able to operate at all (Kamalu also makes this point in chapter one of this book). One may add that South Africa is endowed with precious strategic minerals like manganese, vanadium, chromium, and platinum, the continuous supply of which the United States may want to preserve. One should also not ignore America's huge investment in South Africa that should be protected.

However, all these arguments have been countered. For instance, *The Report of the Study Commission on U.S. Policy Toward Southern Africa* (1981:391) pointed out that strong cooperation with the South African government was not an important factor in protecting the Cape sea route. It noted that although there is an advantage for ships to utilize the calmer seas and shorter passage by traveling close to the Cape itself, it could be avoided, if necessary. This could be done by having ships use the long stretch of navigable water between the Cape and Antarctica. By so doing, the South African Navy, its surveillance and logistical facilities will be marginalized and, hence, become less important elements in keeping the Cape route open.

In regard to the so-called strategic minerals, the report indicated that their uses fall under different categories of importance. "Some are vital to military preparedness, others are economically but not strategically significant and some are merely convenient" (1981:391). More importantly, the report maintained that South Africa's refusal to export these minerals to the United States is likely to be "partial, intermittent and short term...in duration. Medium-term and long-term...interruptions appear unlikely" (1981:392).

Thus, if such reasoning holds, and given the decline of the Soviet Union in global affairs, one may argue that both the United States and the West had no strategic interest in South Africa. What they might have wanted, however, was a peaceful change from institutionalized Apartheid to stability and peace in the Southern African region. This was necessary in order to facilitate and sustain economic and trade relations.

CONSTRUCTIVE ENGAGEMENT

When the Reagan Administration first took office in 1981, there was an apparent shift in the direction and substance of the United States' policy towards South Africa. Ronald Reagan's conservative and pro-status quo stance moved him to put aside Jimmy Carter's appeal for full participation of black South Africans in the political process of their country, an appeal that was grounded on concerns for human rights and in line with United States idealism. Reagan, who had taken issue with Carter for "ignoring vital United States' interests while naively pursuing idealistic human rights goals" (*The Washington Post* June 16, 1981), was not inclined to pursue Carter's confrontational and activist public campaign to pressure the Pretoria government to change its racial policies. Placing more premium on the strategic and military importance of South Africa to United States Cold War defense planning, Reagan moved to improve the strained relations between the United States and South Africa as a component of his global strategy to combat Soviet influence.

From the very beginning, Reagan proclaimed the unequivocal message that he wanted to "open a new chapter" with Pretoria. In March 1981, in an interview with former Columbia Broadcasting Services (CBS) news anchorman Walter Cronkite, Reagan called South Africa a friendly nation that "has stood beside us in every war..., a country that strategically is essential to the free World...(and) has production of minerals we all must have" (*The Washington Post* June 16, 1981).

South African government officials were very much encouraged by Reagan's public expressions about their country and his new approach to the problem in South Africa. As one South African official noted, "not only is it virtually the opposite of that (the policy) adopted by the Carter Government, but it is even more friendly than the policy of Richard Nixon" (*The Washington Post* June 16, 1981).

After a meeting with Pik Botha, South Africa's Foreign Minister at the time, in Washington in May 1981, the Reagan Administration officially announced its policy of "Constructive Engagement." Like the "Containment Policy," constructive engagement was based on an academic assessment of the political reality of the South African situation. It was based on Chester Crocker's analysis of the developments and objective conditions in South Africa in the late 1970s which resulted in the paper "South Africa: Strategy for Change," he published in *Foreign Affairs*, Winter 1980/1981.

As Assistant Secretary of State for African Affairs in the Reagan Administration, Crocker could be said to have been almost solely responsible for formulating, adopting, and implementing constructive engagement. Constructive engagement was meant to establish a cordial and accommodating intercourse with the South African government. The expectation was that through "communication," rather than confrontation, the United States government would be able to influence and entice South Africa's government to implement reforms that would lead to black participation in the political process in South Africa. Also, it was hoped that through cooperation with South Africa, Namibia would become independent,

Soviet influence in Southern Africa would be halted, and stability in the region would be enhanced.

Chester Crocker's strategy of cooperation, rather than confrontation with the Pretoria government, was based on certain key assumptions. First of all, he tended to believe that the South African government under Pieter W. Botha's leadership was a "modernizing autocracy" bent on reform. This thinking could be particularly based on Botha's statement in 1979, in which he indicated that South African whites must "adapt or die." It is also tied to his assertion that he would take the necessary steps to bring about a sustained improvement in American-South African relations. Vivid manifestations of the latter included the initiation of obvious internal reforms, accepting Namibian independence and developing accommodating relations with South Africa's neighbors. Crocker's strategy was also based on the assumption that Reagan had given the United States new credibility because of his pronouncements about extending cordial bilateral relations with Pretoria.

One may note, however, that constructive engagement was more or less National Security Study Memorandum (NSSM)-39 revisited. NSSM-39 was a document that resulted in a review organized by Henry Kissinger, then National Security Adviser under Nixon, to change both the style and substance of American relations with South Africa. Out of five policy options that were recommended by a committee set up for that purpose, Option Two was adopted. This policy option provided that the American government relax its stance towards the ruling white establishment in South Africa, so as to encourage it to make some modifications (reforms) on its racial and "colonial" policies. Like constructive engagement, NSSM-39 called for a closer association with the South African government in an effort to entice it to reform its political system. And that constructive change in South Africa could only result through the acquiescence of the whites themselves. Both policies stressed the economic and strategic interests of the United States while de-emphasizing the most crucial and vital concerns of the political and human rights of black South Africans. This is clearly implied in the recommendations of NSSM-39 when it states: "our tangible interests form a basis for our contacts in the region, and these can be maintained at an acceptable political cost" (see *South Africa: Time Running Out* 1981:351-352).

IMPLEMENTING CONSTRUCTIVE ENGAGEMENT

In response to its policy of constructive engagement, the Reagan Administration started off with overtures to the South African government. For example, in March of 1981, just two months after Reagan took office, South African military officers, including high-level intelligence officers, arrived in Washington to consult with their American counterparts. The Reagan Administration also authorized additional South African honorary consuls in the United States and granted visas to a South African rugby team. Moreover, it relaxed controls over non-lethal exports that the South African military and police could use. The Reagan government also adopted a more flexible attitude towards the sale of dual-use military equipment and sophisticated technology. It even re-established the exchange of military attaches between Washington and Pretoria.

The new Administration was very instrumental in helping the South African government secure a $1.1 billion loan from the International Monetary Fund (IMF) to address its (South African government) ever-increasing balance-of-payment problems, brought about largely by a sharp decline in South Africa's exports and the price of gold. The Reagan Administration supported and continued to help the South African government secure the loan amid strong opposition from many black and liberal white Americans who had argued that such a loan "would subsidize apartheid policies that seriously distort the country's economy and hamper development of its vast resources" (Gray 1982).

Additionally, Chester Crocker never met with South African black leaders or addressed their political concerns. This was mainly because of the Reagan Administration's policy of being cordial and encouraging to the Pretoria government. If Crocker or Reagan himself had met with South African black leaders or openly addressed their concerns, the South African government may not have liked it and would have moved away from implementing reforms toward political and social change. This, in effect, would have foiled the Reagan Administration's game-plan towards South Africa.

In the spirit of constructive engagement, the Reagan Administration turned a blind eye to South Africa's aggression and campaigns of destabilization in the Southern African region. It was silent on South African aggression against neighboring countries like Mozambique and Angola, in spite of its strong and active condemnation of international terrorism. For example, in December 1983, South Africa invaded Angola. Its artillery and bombers struck about 200 miles deep into Angola in an attempt to cripple South West Africa Peoples Organization (SWAPO) operations, and the Reagan Administration said nothing.

Indeed, a constitutional reform in 1983 by Botha called for the establishment of a three-chamber parliament made up of racially-segregated houses for whites, colored, and Indians. Quite obviously, this reform excluded Africans who comprised some 72 percent of the South African population. Such an unfair and unjust reform, for example, was regarded as "a positive step" by the Reagan Administration.

CRITICISMS AND CALLS FOR SANCTIONS AGAINST SOUTH AFRICA

By 1982, the utility and effectiveness of constructive engagement was being called into question. The general feeling in the United States Congress, then, was that the policy had failed to achieve its immediate objective of a Namibian settlement. Most importantly, constructive engagement was not seen as being able to have any impact on the Botha Government in regard to the political rights of blacks. A number of bills and resolutions condemning South African and American policies, and calls for varying degrees of sanctions, were introduced in Congress. In spite of these criticisms, Chester Crocker and the Reagan Administration were able to manage the shortcomings and doubts about constructive engagement in their first term in office. The Reagan Administration brokered the Lusaka agreement between South Africa and Angola, and the Nkomati Accord between South Africa and Mozambique. These were seen as indications that constructive engagement was making strides.

Nonetheless, the latter half of 1984, and especially Reagan's second term in office, witnessed the decline and eventual demise of constructive engagement. This demise increased in pace on September 3, 1984 when South Africa's "no black representation" constitution went into effect. Violent protests broke out in some of the African townships in South Africa. There were also protests in the United States, especially in Washington. Rallies and demonstrations were staged in front of the South African embassy by African American leaders like Randall Robinson, Executive Director of Trans-Africa, Walter Fauntroy, former District of Columbia delegate to Congress, and others (refer to Kimaru's discussion of these developments in chapter three). There were intensive appeals for sanctions and divestment from almost all groups in the American Society. By 1985, series of divestment legislation were passed in six states with fourteen others considering similar measures.

It was, however, Botha's "Rubicon" speech of 1984, in which he indicated there would be no power sharing with blacks in South Africa, that brought about tremendous anti-Apartheid response and divestment from American corporations, banks, schools, etc. This eventually led to the United States Congress enacting the Comprehensive Anti-Apartheid Act of 1986. This legislation "imposed the strongest set of sanctions yet taken against Pretoria by one of its major Western trading partners..." (Baker 1989:45). This Act banned new investments and bank loans to South Africa; stopped South Africa's air links with the United States; prohibited importation of South African products such as coal, uranium, steel, textiles, and agricultural products to the United States; and threatened to cut off military aid to allies suspected of breaching the international arms embargo against South Africa (Baker 1989). This watershed legislation not only contributed to the detrimental effect of sanctions against the South African economy, it also forced the government to make concessions such as lifting the ban on the African National Congress (ANC) and releasing Nelson Mandela from prison. It also set the stage for negotiations for power-sharing in South Africa.

It is worth noting, however, that it was as a result of Reagan's indifference or refusal to impose serious sanctions against the South African government for its atrocities (both in South Africa and its neighboring states), and Pretoria's lethargy towards implementing reforms that would give political rights to blacks in South Africa, which pushed the American Congress to move and enact the Comprehensive Anti-Apartheid legislation (see Kimaru's discussion in chapter three for more on this subject). In essence, the United States Congress seemed to have taken the responsibility to make America's policy towards South Africa from the hands of the Reagan Administration.

Indeed, the Comprehensive Anti-Apartheid Act "set forth a...complete framework to guide the efforts of the United States in helping to bring an end to Apartheid in South Africa and led to the establishment of a non-racial, democratic form of government" (Baker 1989:45). In other words, the Anti-Apartheid Act not only legally called for the replacement of constructive engagement, it also provided guidelines to enhance a stable Southern Africa and a democratic South Africa.

THE BUSH ADMINISTRATION AND SOUTH AFRICA

George Bush was elected president in late 1988 and his administration took office in early 1989. Shortly after his election, some African leaders, who were not pleased with Reagan's pro-Pretoria policy of constructive engagement and its impact on promoting fundamental change in South Africa, called on Bush to change the policy. Zimbabwe's Foreign Minister, Nathan Shamuyarira, for instance, while addressing an anti-Apartheid conference sponsored by the World Council of Churches in Harare on November 21, 1988, urged Bush to discard the Reagan Administration's policy of constructive engagement toward South Africa (see *Africa Report* January-February 1989). He also appealed to Bush to change his approach so that the United States can be seen as actively opposed to South Africa's Apartheid system, supportive of the majority-ruled frontline states, and more importantly, represent a true bearer of democratic ideals by working seriously to see the demise of the Apartheid system.

Even the quasi-governmental *Herald* newspaper in Harare was quoted as urging the incoming Bush Administration to significantly toughen its policy towards South Africa and not "to slavishly follow the soft Reagan line on South Africa, as it will produce nothing but conflict" (*Africa Report* January-February 1989:16). The paper was further quoted as suggesting that in order to move out of the Reagan "shadow," the Bush Administration should support punitive sanctions against South Africa (1989:16).

Nevertheless, it is worth pointing out at this juncture that Reagan's approach to Pretoria toughened by the end of his eight-year term, especially with the enactment of the Comprehensive Anti-Apartheid legislation. Also, constructive engagement as a policy was never abandoned after this legislation (or even after the report of the former Secretary of State, George Shultz, Advisory Committee was submitted to Reagan). The policy, which advocated cooperation with the South African government to promote peaceful change, was still in vogue.

The Bush Administration, at its inception, did not have a comprehensive and clearly defined official policy towards South Africa unlike its predecessor. All that was said was that it had "Basic Principles of U.S. Policy toward South Africa" (Cohen 1989), or an "Emerging U.S. Policy" (Perkins 1989). This was nothing more than a restatement of the cardinal guidelines of a succeeding policy to constructive engagement recommended by the Secretary of State's Advisory Committee on South Africa and created by Reagan in September

1985. Edward Perkins, for instance, in his Department of State Bulletin, "New Dimensions in U.S. Foreign Policy," asserted the following:

1. We should continue to press the South African government for fundamental political change

2. We should continue to condemn the South African government's systematic violation of human rights.

3. We should continue to vigorously support black political and economic empowerment, plus provide scholarships for black students (see *Current Policy* no. 1253).

These policy stances can also be found in A *U.S. Policy Toward South Africa*, a report released by the Shultz Advisory Committee.

In practice, the Bush Administration was, to a very large extent, following the recommendations of the Shultz Advisory Committee. Thus, it pursued the policies that the Reagan Administration had already started to enforce, policies that were not only favorably directed at the Pretoria government but to the anti-Apartheid leaders as well. For instance, after the enforcement of the comprehensive anti-Apartheid legislation, we witnessed, for the first time, the Reagan Administration pursuing greater contact or "engagement" with the ANC and other anti-Apartheid organizations. A rapport engineered by the former United States ambassador to South Africa, Edward Perkins, culminated in a meeting between the late ANC President, Oliver Tambo, and former American Secretary of State, George Shultz, in January 1987.

The Bush Administration also pursued a policy of closer engagement with blacks and anti-Apartheid leaders. One of Bush's first moves when he took office was to invite Albertina Sisulu, the wife of Walter Sisulu, and her associates in the United Democratic Front (UDF) to the White House. Bush also extended invitation to Nelson Mandela shortly after he was released from prison in February 1990. In fact, Bush met with Nelson Mandela, Chief Mangosuthu Buthelezi, and other key South African political leaders including former President de Klerk.

Another area in which one could see a continuation of Reagan's policy in the Bush Administration was that of sanctions. The Bush Administration, like the Reagan Administration, was opposed to sanctions. This was mainly due to the fact that the Bush Administration believed that even though sanctions had affected the thinking of the Pretoria government, its implementation would only result in hurting South Africa's neighbors and blacks in South Africa.

However, the Bush Administration, unlike the Reagan Administration, was very tactful in handling the issue of sanctions with Congress. A bipartisan consensus was created between the Bush Administration and the United States Congress in dealing with the South African issue. This was brought about through intensive consultations with various groups in Congress, the Black Caucus, and other members of the Bush Administration, including James Baker and Herman Cohen. Such an effort not only resulted in a working relationship between the Bush Administration and the white establishment in South Africa, it also won credibility with the black masses and their leaders in that country.

It is important to note that a concrete manifestation of the Bush Administration's bipartisan effort was the conclusion of an agreement between the executive branch and Congress in 1989 to hold off implementing more sanctions against South Africa's government for about six to nine months. This was to provide the de Klerk government with some time to institute meaningful reforms toward the achievement of a racial-free democratic South Africa.

Also, unlike the Reagan Administration, the Bush Administration was quite open in decrying Apartheid. For example, on his visit to Soweto, South Africa, on Friday, March 23, 1990, American Secretary of State, James Baker, not only expressed his distaste for the abject poverty in the township, but also openly said that South Africa's policy of racial separation must be abolished as quickly as possible (see *The Washington Post*, March 1990:A-33).

Indeed, the Bush Administration, unlike the Reagan Administration, was relatively more willing to meet with members of the ANC. For example, even though Mandela had refused to meet with Baker in South Africa at an earlier date, Baker was willing to hold a 30-minute talk with Mandela in Windhoek, Namibia, on March 21, 1990—Namibia's day of independence from South Africa. Also, on his visit to South Africa on March 23, 1990, Baker was guided around the township of Soweto by Walter Sisulu, the principal organizer inside South Africa of the ANC. Baker even had breakfast with Sisulu at his modest cottage on the same day (*The Washington Post*, March 1990:A-33). The Bush Administration was also very instrumental in setting the stage for talks or negotiations between blacks and whites by not only having talks with de Klerk, but with other anti-Apartheid groups as well.

It may not be erroneous for one to suggest that the Bush Administration was relatively more "constructive" in its engagement in South Africa than the Reagan Administration. Bush was not only tactful and conciliatory in his approach, he was very pragmatic as well. He opened lines of communication with both blacks and whites in South Africa and established a bipartisan consensus with Congress.

Perhaps, a major reason why the Bush Administration was so practical in its policy towards South Africa, and refrained from a clear-cut, articulate policy, is because it wanted to avoid a confrontation with Congress—a confrontation that the Reagan Administration faced and led Congress to take tangible steps to bring about the end of Apartheid. Besides, the South African situation had become an explosive domestic political issue in the United States. In addition, South Africa had also become a human rights issue in the United States and not so much a strategic or economic one.

President Bush indeed enjoyed the fruits of Ronald Reagan's labor. He not only saw the independence of Namibia (Crocker's constructive linkage), but also the "talks about talks" of a post-Apartheid South Africa—a result of the work of the Reagan Advisory Committee on South Africa.

Conclusion

In the above pages, a discussion of United States foreign policy towards South Africa during the Reagan-Bush era is presented. It can be seen that the goal of American foreign policy had been largely twofold: (1) that of promoting, defending, and safeguarding democratic principles and economic development world-wide; (2) that of deterring communist expansion.

Reagan's initial policy of constructive engagement was not specifically directed at the main issues in the region, that of peacefully abolishing Apartheid, enhancing Namibia's independence, as well as ensuring stability in the Southern African region. With constructive engagement, Reagan revived the Cold War rivalry and made anti-communism the guiding principle of American policy towards South Africa. Hence, Reagan spent more time praising Botha's token changes and turning a blind eye to his (Botha's) atrocities both at home and in neighboring states in Southern Africa. Soviet expansionism, rather than racism or human rights, took precedence in the constructive engagement policy. It, therefore, failed!

Another major reason constructive engagement failed, especially under Reagan, was because in its implementation, it was not directed purposefully at the main issues of racism, black political rights, Namibia's independence and political stability in Southern Africa. But when attention was focused on these issues, following the passage of the Comprehensive Anti-Apartheid Act of 1986 and the implementation of the recommendations of the Secretary of State's Advisory Committee on South Africa, changes started taking place. Thus, the preceding explanation goes a long way to substantiate the thesis that constructive engagement failed to achieve its objectives because it was not purposefully directed at solving the issues at hand, but was made a secondary element to the Cold War rivalry.

The Bush Administration's policy towards South Africa was not clearly defined and articulated like Reagan's constructive engagement. In fact, one may say that Bush's foreign policy towards South Africa was based on a "wait and see" approach or, more specifically, that of implementing the recommendations of the Reagan's Advisory Committee on South Africa. Bush's policy towards South Africa, in practice, was relatively more "constructive" than that of Reagan because while he (Bush) talked to both black and white parties of the conflict, Reagan only devoted his attention and support to the white South African government. Also, the Bush Administration was quite open and bold in condemning the South African Government and its Apartheid policy while Reagan lavished on that government "false" praises for token reforms.

The reforms that took place under de Klerk's Administration, the freeing of Nelson Mandela and other ANC leaders, the repeal of the 1986 state of emergency regulation, the unbanning of political parties in South Africa following de Klerk's speech to parliament on February 2, 1990, the repeal of the Population Registration Act and Group Areas Act in June 1990, and the negotiations that took place between the former South African government and black South African leaders were positive steps toward the achievement of a race-neutral, democratic South Africa. These were part of the conditions that the South African government had to meet to warrant the lifting of sanctions placed on it by section 311 of the Comprehensive Anti-Apartheid Act of 1986. In fact, for implementing the aforementioned reforms on July 10, 1991, President Bush signed Executive Order 12769 terminating sanctions against South Africa.

ENDNOTES

1. This plan came into effect in 1948. It was the United States government's solution to revive Western Germany and other European economies after their devastation by the Second World War. The plan itself was to provide European countries with huge grants to enable them to stand on their own economic feet and play an active part in international trade.

2. The fear that the Soviet Union would occupy the political vacuum created by Britain's withdrawal of guarantees of Turkey and Greece caused the Truman Administration to implement a plan that would "help free people to maintain their institutions and their integrity against aggressive movements that seek to impose upon them totalitarian regimes" (cited in Kennedy 1987:372). In accordance with this plan, the Truman Administration supplied military equipment and professional military advisers to Greece and Turkey in 1947. They were, thus, both saved from Soviet communist domination.

3. The United States was involved in both wars to prevent communist expansion.

4. The United States participated in the production of strategic arms with the Soviet Union in order to prevent that country from accumulating strategic weapons that would threaten world stability.

Chapter Three

American Lobby Groups and the Shaping of United States Policies toward Africa

Chris M. Kimaru

INTRODUCTION

This chapter focuses on American lobby groups and the role that they play in shaping United States policies toward Africa. The first section begins by examining the role that lobbying plays in United States policy making. The influence and growth of lobby groups are then examined. The section after that attempts to tie United States interests in Africa to the various pressure groups that lobby the government for these interests and try to influence American policies toward Africa in their favor. These interests are examined at length, along with the effectiveness of the lobby groups in influencing United States policies toward the African continent. The final section focuses on Washington lobby firms that have become quite popular with African governments that often want to cut through red tape and get their issues to American policy makers quickly. Before doing all this, a brief background on the issue is in order.

The United States news media often portray Africa as a continent laden with problems. It is true that Africa has its share of problems, which include natural disasters, illiteracy, famine, malnutrition, infectious diseases, ravages of war, political oppression, corruption and human rights abuses. One only needs to open a newspaper or watch news on television to encounter reports on these problems. The news reports, however, do not tell us that these problems are not unique, nor are they confined to the African continent.

The news reports are sometimes too sensationalized to be informative. The correspondents come across as blaming the victim rather than reporting and analyzing the problems. They usually are not as keen on reporting on United States inaction and often late response to human suffering. When the US finally decides to join other Western aid donors in helping the hungry, the drought stricken, and the war torn, help usually arrives late after many lives have been lost, as in the case of Somalia and more recently Rwanda.

During the Cold War, there was even a better excuse to turn away from African problems especially if the African country was labeled as communist. A case in point is Ethiopia in 1984, where famine had contributed to the death of at least 300,000 people, with an additional one million expected to perish before the disaster was over (*Newsweek* November 26, 1984:54). The United States was reluctant to help and was very slow in responding to the crisis. Ethiopia's status as a Soviet ally inhibited the Reagan Administration's effort. In the words of Patrick Leahy of Vermont, the hungry Ethiopian kids were seen as "little commies" (*Newsweek* November 26, 1984:54) and for this reason the administration dragged its feet.

But why should the United States care about what happens to Africa? The answer to this question can be answered by yet another question. Why should it not? The United States has cared deeply about problems in Europe, the ancestral home of the white majority, to the extent that it went to war to protect many of those countries against a tyrant that threatened domination over them. After the war, European countries were destitute from the ravages of the war. Once again, the United States came to their aid and helped them rebuild their economies through the Marshall Plan, which provided a substantial $17 billion toward the rebuilding (see Bangura's lengthy discussion about the Marshall Plan in chapter four).

The United States is often said to be a melting pot made up of people from different races and nationalities. Given this ethnic and racial mix one can argue that to be fair to the various groups in this country, compassion shown to the ancestral home of the majority should also be extended to the ancestral home of the minority groups.

But that still begs the question: Why is this compassion and caring not extended to the ancestral home of African Americans who make up 13% of the American population? Why haven't we heard of a Marshall Plan for Africa or an American $10 billion loan guarantee to resettle the millions of Africans displaced by the ravages of war, especially in Rwanda, Burundi, Angola, Ethiopia, Mozambique, Somalia, and the Sudan?

The Jewish population, by contrast, comprises a much smaller percentage of the United States population; and yet, the State of Israel receives $3 billion in aid every year, making Israel the largest recipient of American aid (*The Washington Post* January 2, 1990). The move by the late Israeli Prime Minister Yitzhak Rabin to freeze construction of new settlements in the Israeli-occupied territories removed the obstacle that caused the Bush Administration to object to approving the $10 billion loan guarantees that Israel sought to help settle immigrants from the former Soviet Union (*US News and World Report* August 17, 1992). A $10 billion loan guarantee coupled with a $3 billion in aid is surely generous and shows real compassion for Israel.

But why is there such a wide disparity in compassion and caring, measured here in terms of dollars expended in a concerted effort to alleviate the problems of a people? Are Jewish Americans favored over other groups because Israel gets a lion's share of United States aid? Or, should credit go to the American-Israel Public Affairs Committee (AIPAC), the influential Israel lobby, which pressures Congress into appropriating billions of dollars in aid to Israel every year?

Of course, credit should go to AIPAC for its magnificent lobbying efforts for the state of Israel. Smith (1988:217) traces the history of AIPAC's strong influence from 1981, when the lobby group lost a fight over the Reagan Administration's decision to sell AWACS (Air Warning and Control Systems) planes to Saudi Arabia. This loss jolted AIPAC into a political strategy to transform itself into a super lobby. To accomplish this, AIPAC increased its membership from nine thousand households in 1978 to fifty-five thousand in 1987. By the mid-1980s, AIPAC was steering roughly $4 million in campaign contributions to friendly candidates and punishing political foes.

The political payoff was evident in the tremendous increase in American aid to Israel from $93.4 million in 1962 to nearly $3.8 billion in 1986. AIPAC had also gained so much political muscle that by 1985, the organization and its allies forced President Reagan to renege on an arms deal he had promised King Hussein of Jordan. In 1987, AIPAC's lobbying efforts blocked the sale of 1,600 maverick missiles to Saudi Arabia. Also, AIPAC successfully lobbied the Bush Administration to drop its objection to approving the $10 billion loan guarantee that Israel wanted to help settle immigrants from the former Soviet Union. Senator Robert Dole of Kansas must have had this lobby in mind when he asked "Pressure Groups" to relax their stranglehold on Congress (*The New York Times* January 16, 1990). To determine the role played by such lobby groups as AIPAC and others, it is important to examine the influence that such lobby groups have in the shaping of United States policies toward other countries.

LOBBYING AND UNITED STATES POLICY MAKING

To fully comprehend public policy making in the United States, it is important to understand the role that interest groups play in shaping of such policies. Interest groups have been very effective in getting problems to government or getting issues on what political scientists call the "institutional agenda." Of course, groups such as the American Medical Association (AMA) and the National Rifle Association (NRA), which command considerable financial and organizational resources, have more success in tilting public policies in their favor than the resource-starved and poorly-organized groups.

Interest groups in America, as Graham (1990:3) observes, provide an alternative form of political participation to voting or membership of a political party and may, in certain respects, provide a superior form of participation. Interest groups help in raising issues that are too detailed or specialized to be the concern of political parties or central in election campaigns. Thus, interest groups allow intense minorities; that is, groups vitally affected by a policy issue to prevail over majorities to whom the issue matters little.

Berry (1989:6) lists the roles played by interest groups as: (1) to represent their constituents before government; (2) to afford people the opportunity to participate in the political process; (3) to educate the American public about political issues; (4) to get involved in agenda building, which basically turns problems into issues that become part of the body of policy questions that government feels it must deal with (institutional agenda); (5) to monitor programs to make sure that they deliver to their constituents what they were intended to deliver, and that program implementation is in compliance with the law.

Participation in American interest group politics increased significantly in the 1980s, as these groups continued to replace political parties as the dominant organizations of American politics. Hrebenar and Scott (1990) describe this sharp decline of political parties and the related rise of interest groups as articulators of political demands as the "era of new politics."

There are many terms used to denote organizations that are involved in lobbying to affect public policy decisions. Such terms as "pressure groups" and "special interest groups" have acquired a negative connotation because they are viewed as self-serving and not concerned about public interest at large. The term "interest group," though not devoid of this negative connotation, is seen as somewhat neutral and will be used interchangeably with the term "lobby group" in this chapter.

An interest group can be said to be engaging in *lobbying*, if it attempts to influence policy makers. Actually, the word lobby comes from the practice of interest group representatives standing in the lobbies of legislatures so that they could stop members on their way to a session for a quick discussion of the merits or demerits of a bill.

Truman (1971:33) defines an interest group as any group that is based on one or more shared attitudes and makes certain claims upon other groups or organizations in the society. Making those claims upon other groups or organizations involves lobbying.

Lobbying can be used as a technique for gaining legislative support or other institutional approval for a given objective. The objective could be a policy shift, a judicial ruling, or the modification or passage of a law. Mahood (1990:53) points out that lobbying is also employed to reinforce support for established policies or it can be used to activate allies for defensive purposes, especially to oppose a policy shift and maintain the political status quo.

Hrebenar and Scott (1990:2) use the 1987 Judge Robert Bork confirmation hearings to show how lobby groups can affect policy decisions in America. More than 185 liberal organizations opposed Judge Bork. Among the notable organizations were Norman Lear's People for the American Way (PAW), the AFL-CIO, the National Organization of Women (NOW), the National Abortion Rights Action League (NAAL), the National Association for the Advancement of Colored People (NAACP) Legal Defense and Educational Fund.

Judge Bork's conservative support was quite strong and included such groups as the American Conservative Union (ACU), Concerned Women for America (CWA), the National Rights to Work Committee (NRWC) and such influential television evangelists as Reverend Jerry Falwell of the Moral Majority, Dr. Robert Grant of the Christian Voice, and Pat Robertson of the 700 Club. The liberal interest groups waged a skillful fight to defeat the nomination. Actually, the loss in the full Senate by a record vote of 58 to 42 was an impressive victory credited to the liberal interest groups.

The liberal interest groups' victory should be balanced with the 1991 nomination of Judge Clarence Thomas to the Supreme Court against much opposition from some of the same liberal interest groups. Judge Thomas' confirmation by the Senate by one of the narrowest margins in history (52-48) was much more involved than the Bork nomination because women as a group played a significant role in pressuring their senators to vote against Judge Thomas. Such senators as Joseph I. Liebermann of Connecticut, Richard H. Bryan and Harry Reid of Nevada, who had been solid supporters of the Judge during the hearings ended up voting "No." They were joined by three other Democrats who initially had hinted that they supported Judge Thomas—Bob Graham of Florida, Daniel Patrick Moynihan of New York, and Robert C. Byrd of West Virginia (*The New York Times* October 16, 1991).

So, even though it was a victory for the conservatives, it was a narrow victory that could have gone the other way had three more senators caved in under pressure and voted against Judge Thomas. That case would have given the liberals yet another victory.

The Judges Bork and Thomas hearings are just two examples of how different lobby groups can get intensely involved in an issue or nomination that they feel could affect their members, favorably or unfavorably. Lobbying in Washington is big business and all sectors of the economy are represented.

Big business has numerous representatives in Washington, but most businesses and corporations also belong to such umbrella groups as the powerful National Association of Manufacturers (NAM) and the United States Chamber of Commerce (USCC). The USCC, founded in 1912 to be the major voice for business interests in America, is the largest and best known group in America. The Chamber grew out of the insecurity which pervaded the business world in the period immediately preceding World War I. Businesses saw themselves threatened not only by labor, but also by the federal government. Instances of such presumably hostile attitudes were the passage of the Sherman and Clayton (Antitrust) Acts, the vigorous prosecution of trusts (large corporations controlling certain industries) by the Theodore Roosevelt Administration, and the growing demands of disadvantaged groups for increased regulation of business (Ziegler and Peak 1972:229).

Business groups recognize that government action, whether in the form of economic policy, monetary policy, or regulatory policy, directly affects their performance in the market and the economy at large. Thus, they will actively lobby to influence such government policies in their favor. Hrebenar and Scott (1990:263) cite the 1977 lobbying effort by the American Telephone and Telegraphy Company (AT&T) for passage of a communications bill that would discourage competition in the telephone business, to show how big businesses can aggressively push their cases in Congress to tilt the legislative scale in their favor. AT&T in this endeavor beefed up its push for the bill with expenditures of over $2.5 million during the 1976-1977 legislative year.

Organized labor has been a major lobbying force in American politics since the mid 1950s, when the AFL and CIO merged into a powerful labor union (AFL-CIO) and lobby, representing millions of skilled and unskilled workers. Labor continues to invest heavily in candidates deemed to be "friendly to workers." Even though labor's endorsed candidates in the 1980 and 1984 presidential elections were not elected, an AFL-CIO endorsement still carries much weight and is well sought after. Most of the work involved in getting political influence is done by the AFL-CIO's political arm, COPE (Committee on Political Education), which spends millions of dollars in each election year on contributions to candidates, registration drives, encouraging voters to vote and educating them on political issues deemed crucial by labor.

Farmers, who make up about two percent (2%) of the nation's population, are represented by a large number of agricultural groups. But the two major farm lobbies are the American Farm Bureau (AFB), which represents the wealthy, and the National Farmers Union (NFU), which represents the lower income farmer. AFB favors a limited economic role for government, whereas NFU favors government intervention and support for farm products.

The professional organizations are also well represented in Washington. Two of the most influential groups in this category are the American Medical (AMA) and the National Education Association (NEA). These two groups launched very intensive lobbying campaigns especially in the 1992 presidential election where a number of issues of concern to these two groups were at stake.

One of the issues that is currently at stake is the national health policy which is going through a reformulation stage. AMA is opposed to compulsory national health insurance and hospital control legislation and intensively lobbies against such legislations. The AMA leads all other individual interest groups in money given to elected officials and often heads the list in the distribution of political money in elections. The AMA led the donations list with $1.4 million in contributions in 1974, increased to $1.7 million in 1976, and a first-place contribution of $1.6 million to congressional and senate candidates in 1978 (Hoebenat and Scott 1990:276). The AMA's intensity as a lobby group to influence the national health policy can be demonstrated by its strong campaign against Medicare. It reported spending between $7 million and $12 million in 1962 to fight Medicare (Dekin 1966:222).

In addition to professional associations, there are religious groups, ethnic groups, racial groups, pro- or anti-abortion groups, veterans associations, gay and lesbian groups, and feminist groups. The list of those represented is long and includes even welfare recipients who are represented by the National Welfare Rights Organization (NWRO), which was formed in the 1960s to lobby for increased federal welfare programs.

Ornstein and Elder (1978:29) argue that ethnic cultural groups such as AHEPA (the Greek American cultural association), the Italian American Foundation (IAF), and the Polish American Congress (PAC), as well as groups like B'nai B'rith, the Knights of Columbus, and the National Association for the Advancement of Colored People (NAACP) serve in part to reinforce their members' identification with ethnic, religious, or racial backgrounds.

It is important to note, however, that emphasis of these ethnic cultural groups has shifted to lobbying for or against issues that affect their members. For example, rather than focus on ethnic identification, NAACP lobbies for such issues as civil rights and increased funding for inner cities which are important for its members. The American-Israel Public Affairs Committee (AIPAC), discussed earlier, also falls under this category; but the emphasis of its activities has been lobbying for the State of Israel, which its Jewish members consider a top priority issue.

Lobbying, as can be seen, has become an important vehicle for getting problems to government and for influencing public policy. Lobbying is not limited only to organized domestic groups. Individual citizens are known to lobby Congress for passage or defeat of legislation that they consider important to their interests. For example, Texas billionaire and former presidential candidate, Ross Perot, hired a lobbyist to influence Congress to enact an amendment to the Internal Revenue Code that would have had the effect of reducing Perot's tax liability (US Congress 1977:97).

Foreign governments are also well represented in Washington. Ornstein and Elder state the following:

> Virtually every foreign nation of significant size has a lobbying agent or agents operating in Washington. Many foreign agents are prominent political figures. They lobby Congress and the State Department on such diverse issues as military aid, most-favored-nation trade status, and allowing the concord supersonic airplane to land and take off in the United States (1978:51).

Representation by a lobbyist is considered crucial because lobbyists can gain access to key policy makers and win their confidence. They are knowledgeable and have the requisite bargaining and technical skills. They have the ability and the skills to put their client's case on the front burner. In the words of Edward Rollins, former White House Aide to President Reagan and Co-Chairman to the Ross Perot failed presidential campaign, "I've got many, many friends who are all through the agencies and equally important, I don't have many enemies...I tell my clients I can get your case moved to the top of the pile" (*National Journal* 1986:1052).

The next part of this chapter focuses on lobby groups that are involved in shaping United States policies toward Africa. A number of the more affluent African countries have lobbyists representing them in Washington, but many of the poorer ones cannot afford the exorbitantly priced services of lobbyists. And considering the limited demands on Washington by many of these countries, the costs easily outweigh the benefits.

AMERICAN LOBBY GROUPS AND AFRICA

To understand American lobby groups' involvement in Africa, one must first understand what the United States interests are in that region. It is in the pursuit of those interests and sometimes personal gains that propel lobby groups to get involved in influencing policies. It is important to note here that American lobby group involvement in Africa is a recent phenomenon. Before 1960, most African countries were under colonial rule. As such, direct American interactions with them was minimal, and they ranked low in United States foreign policy considerations.

There are a number of explanations given for this. Emerson (1967) argues that the colonial status of most of Africa prior to 1960 prevented the United States from operating freely in the region. The United States had to work through colonial powers that were not ready to authorize extensive American activities in their colonies. McKinley (1974:26) states that the fact that Africa was a European domain was accepted as a fact by Americans. Government officials, scholars, and travelers who thought of Africa could not but think of its European rulers. Most American commentators saw England and France as "the great arbiters of African destiny." To these writers, "the road to Africa" lay "through London and Paris." It can be rightfully argued that the United States has continued to treat some African countries as the exclusive sphere of influence of their former colonizers and has deferred to these European governments in matters that concern these former colonies.

A notable example of this would be the United States taking sides with the French and refusing to come to Guinea's aid after the French pulled out of the country, leaving the country in a destitute and deplorable state in 1958. This was precipitated by a plebiscite, in which Guinea was the only territory among former French colonies to reject the constitution of the Fifth French Republic. Mahoney (1983:36) explains that after Sekou Touré refused France's offer of community status, the French pulled out in a fit of pique taking all administrative records and stripping their colonial offices. They even ripped phones out of the walls. A desperate Sekou Touré appealed to the United States for economic aid. But out of deference to its affronted ally, Washington ignored the request. When Sekou Touré sent another request to Eisenhower for a small amount of military aid, Washington again did not answer. The State Department initially claimed that it had never received the letter, but later admitted that "an irregular request did arrive" (*The New York Times* April 30, 1959).

Sekou Touré was forced to turn to the former eastern bloc for help. When Czechoslovakia, a leading distributor of Soviet weaponry at the time made an unconditional arms offer to Guinea, Touré accepted. By 1960, there were more than 1,500 Soviet and Eastern European technicians in Guinea and Sekou Touré and Nikita Khrushchev were on good terms. So, even though the Eisenhower Administration labeled him a communist "dupe" (*The New York Times* April 30, 1959), Sekou Touré was not bothered because after all it was the communists who came to his aid in his hour of need.

Kitchen (1983:2) summarizes United States national interests in Africa as largely economic and geopolitical. The economic priorities include retaining access to certain critical minerals for the defense-related industries and, to a lesser extent, oil. The geopolitical priorities were to deter hegemonic intrusions by the Soviets or their surrogates into African countries and regions historically linked to the West and to cement "special relationships" with governments willing to provide access to ports and other facilities supportive of a global military outreach (Hill makes this same point in chapter five of this book). Since Cold War hostilities have ceased and the Russians are no longer viewed as the enemy, deterrence of hegemonic intrusions is no longer a top priority in United States national interests in Africa.

Whitaker (1978:60) argues that United States interests intersect with African issues at three main points: (1) in the quest for economic access to Africa's resources and investment opportunities, (2) in the North-South politics in the United Nations and other forms for multilateral negotiations, and (3) in the internalization of African conflicts.

These arguments and others about United States involvement in Africa have economic interest in common. There seems to be a consensus about United States economic interest in Africa a desire to continue to have access to Africa's resources and investment opportunities. Africa could be expanded both as a market and as a source of raw materials, a fact that does not go unnoticed by United States business interests.

We should also not forget that Africa is the ancestral home of African Americans who make up 13% of the United States population. To many of them, Africa is the motherland and the land of their forefathers and foremothers. Rupert Emerson asserts that "the most vital and unique concern of the United States with Africa derives from the existence of that ten percent (now 13%) of the American population originating from Africa." He adds that "the Negro-American has not yet attained the full potential of his ability to influence African American relations. It may be taken for granted that in the coming years both his interest in Africa and his power to do something about it will sharply increase" (1967:52).

Emerson's observation suggests that African Americans have the potential to influence United States policies toward Africa, but have not exploited this potential much. This observation parallels W. E. B. DuBois' criticism of African Americans for waning in their identity with African nationalism in the postwar era. DuBois would have preferred African Americans to play a more active role in shaping United States policy towards the motherland much like other groups were doing for their lands of ancestry. He argued that "When we think of the help which Irish

Americans have given Ireland, and how Scandinavia, Italy, Germany, Poland and China have been aided by their emigrants in the United States, it is tragic that American Negroes today are...doing little to help Africa in its hour of supreme need" (1967:265).

To totally blame African Americans for inaction or apathy as regards United States policies toward Africa would be unfair and inaccurate. Whereas it might be true that a large number of African Americans have been apathetic and indifferent in matters regarding Africa, it is also true that there have always been groups among them working tirelessly to maintain that link with the motherland. This involvement by African Americans has often been dismissed lightly and not put in its proper perspective.

Jackson (1982:142) argues that the earliest organization created by African Americans for the express purpose of influencing United States policies toward Africa was the Council of African Affairs, which was founded in New York in January 1937. The Council was founded less than a year after Italy's invasion of Ethiopia, which for African Americans had been the worldwide symbol of black dignity and power. The Council was interracial, but under black leadership. Among the Council's original twelve members were Max Yergan, a YMCA official with seventeen years of service in African countries and the first black faculty member of the City University of New York; Mordecai W. Johnson, President of Howard University, the nation's leading black institution at the time; Paul Robeson, the world-renowned actor and concert singer; and Ralph J. Bunche, a Professor of Political Science at Howard University who later became Assistant Secretary-General of the United Nations. An important white member was Raymond Leslie Buell of Harvard University, a political scientist with a specialization in African Affairs and a member of the prestigious Foreign Policy Association (FPA). After William Alphaeus Hunton, a brilliant black scholar and a marxist joined in August 1943, the Council developed a radical ideological defense of African liberation. This radicalism rendered the Council vulnerable to the McCarthyism of the 1950s. Actually, even though the Council managed to survive until 1955, Senator Joseph McCarthy's smear of the Council in his anticommunist witch hunts destroyed the Council's credibility and precipitated its demise.

The Council had clearly defined its objectives as follows: (1) to provide concrete assistance to African nationalist struggles; (2) to disseminate accurate information on Africa and African peoples; (3) most significantly, to influence the United States government to adopt policies favorable to

African independence. It also endeavored to swing public opinion behind these goals through press releases, radio programs, mass meetings, and *New Africa*, the organization's monthly publication. Membership rose to two thousand, and the Council's budget jumped from about $11,000 in 1942 to a peak of nearly $40,000 four years later (Lynch 1978:23).

Lynch (1978:17) describes the Council on African Affairs as the longest-lived and most influential American Organization of its kind. Its radical and militant stance, however, did not sit well with Washington. After World War II, Washington's hostility intensified after the Council denounced the Marshall Plan, the North Atlantic Treaty, and the establishment of NATO as mechanisms "to guarantee that colonial people under...(European) rule shall not win their destiny of freedom and independence" (Lynch 1978:42). As mentioned earlier, McCarthyism finally struck the Council on African Affairs a deathblow in 1955.

AMERICAN LOBBY GROUPS AND AFRICA: A CONTEMPORARY RECORD

More recently, another credible, mass-based, black lobby aspiring to influence United States policies toward Africa has arisen in TransAfrica. As a lobby group, TransAfrica seeks to influence United States policies toward Africa and the Caribbean. Jackson (1982:124) states that TransAfrica grew out of a 1976 meeting of 130 blacks summoned by Charles Diggs and Andrew Young (when both were still Congressmen) to challenge Secretary Kissinger's policy on Rhodesia. TransAfrica's founding members were Ronald Walters, a Professor and Chairman of Political Science at Howard University; C. Payne Lukas, Chief Executive Officer of Africare, Inc.; Willard R. Johnson, a scholar and a member of the Council on Foreign Relations; Herschelle Challenor and Randall Robinson, who worked as aides to Diggs, who was Chairman of the House Subcommittee on Africa.

Today, the name of Randall Robinson, the Executive Director of TransAfrica, has become synonymous with the lobby group. Robinson, a graduate of Harvard Law School, is a skilled lobbyist with an insider's knowledge of the American political process, as well as the interest-group focus of American politics. He has skillfully avoided the radical and militant approach of the defunct Council of African Affairs by seeking to influence United States policies toward Africa from within the system. This approach has been quite successful in many instances.

In summarizing the major accomplishments of TransAfrica's lobbying by 1979, Jackson (1982:125) quotes Randall Robinson taking credit for TransAfrica being instrumental in convening the London Conference, which prepared the way for black majority-rule in Zimbabwe and for stopping the United States from lifting the sanctions on trade with Rhodesia, despite Prime Minister Bishop Abel Muzorewa's effort. Robinson also attributed the increased American foreign assistance to Africa and the Caribbean to TransAfrica's lobbying pressure.

TransAfrica has been quite effective in educating African Americans and their leaders in foreign affairs and especially on issues pertaining to Africa and the Caribbean. The lobby group is quite inclusive and works closely with such civil rights organizations as the National Association for the Advancement of Colored People (NAACP) and Jesse Jackson's Rainbow Coalition.

When Congress imposed economic sanctions on South Africa in 1986, Robinson credited the achievement to the African American participation. He reminds us about the following:

> It is important that the world know this particular crack in this particular regime was made, by and large, by Black Americans. Thousands of people who marched outside that embassy, some of whom stood out there every single day for a year. It is vital that African Americans understand the difference they have made (*The Washington Post* March 13, 1990).

The change in terminology, as Emerson wrote, from Negro American to Black American and eventually to African American, is noteworthy. The African American has come to terms with what Emerson (1967:52) calls the denial of the African phase of his heritage. This has happened as a result of increased interaction between African Americans and African people, and better education and information about Africa, which has somewhat helped dispel the Tarzan and Jane and Daktari television myths that most Americans grew up watching. Alex Haley's "Roots" also contributed enormously to educating African Americans about their African heritage. So, despite its many problems, Africa has become a rallying point for black identity. It provides a psychological cloak of protection in the diaspora, including a distinctive heritage of culture and history.

United States interests in Africa can be summarized and grouped into two major areas. The first is economic interest, which is also a concern of the business lobby. The second is the ethnic group interest which stems from the desire by the African American to play a more active role in influencing United States policies toward Africa (see also Bangura's discussion in chapter four).

A third interest, which will be discussed at length later in this chapter, is based on a confluence of interests between the United States and African countries. An earlier study by this author found that the primary interest of giving aid to tropical Africa is to promote American exports (Kimaru 1980). The leaders of the recipient African countries have an interest in receiving aid dollars to supplement their meager national budgets; and also in some cases, to line their pockets, as Mobutu and others like him have done over the years. Incidentally, Zaire's $10 billion debt is the same size as Mobutu's estimated personal fortune (*US News and World Report* August 10, 1992:34). It is obvious that Mobutu's fortune did not come from toil and thrift, but from graft and misappropriation of Zaire's wealth.

These three areas of interest will be addressed individually. The objective is to examine the extent of lobbying activity and the effectiveness of such lobbying in the past.

ECONOMIC INTEREST

American economic interests, mainly in trade and investments, are aimed at maintaining both employment and a high standard of living at home. This point is often echoed in the rhetoric of politicians and especially presidential candidates when they promise to "make America strong again." Simply put, this means making America more economically competitive and increasing American exports abroad. Increased demand for United States exports would, in turn, create more jobs at home.

Pursuing these economic interests is a function of American business with the backing of the United States government. This makes it necessary for the American business lobby to seek to influence government policies that affect trade and business activities abroad. There are numerous examples of involvement of the business lobby in the shaping of policies that affect groups with business interests in Africa.

Ogene (1983:21-38) gives an example of interest group involvement in the United States policy making during the Congo crisis which lasted from 1960 to 1964. The United States policy supported unity in the Congo, but quite a number of groups including the business lobby supported Katanga secession. The business groups supporting Katanga secession had investments in Katanga and South Kasai regions. The two areas were rich in copper, cobalt, tin, industrial diamonds, and other minerals. United States industries which depended on these minerals as raw materials tended to support any political arrangement that would guarantee the security of the sources of supply. These businesses saw the secession of Katanga as assuring such security.

Liberal groups such as the American Committee on Africa, through its organ, *Africa Today*, supported the United States government stand and accused the pro-Katanga lobby of the following:

> Sowing confusion in the minds of many Americans and protested that the lobby had distorted the facts in its *New York Times* advertisement. The prime cause of Katanga's secession was not African tribal dynamics but the mining companies which financed, equipped and organized secession (*Africa Today* February 1962:3).

African American groups and leaders, including James Farmer of the Congress on Racial Equality (CORE); Martin Luther King, Jr., President of the Southern Christian Conference (SCC); Roy A. Wilkins, executive secretary of the National Association for the Advancement of Colored People (NAACP); A. Philip Randolph, President of the Negro-American Labor Council (NALC); and Dorothy Height, President of the National Council of Negro Women (NCNW) all supported the administration's policy and demanded that the United States continue to support the Congo unity (*Africa Today* December 1962:16). This is a case where the business lobby was not successful in influencing policy in its favor. But as Lowi (1964) has noted, the conclusion that interest groups are unimportant in one policy area does not establish that they are unimportant in all areas of policy.

There are instances where the American business lobby has been quite successful. Ogene (1983:102-141) gives an example of the importation of Rhodesian chrome from 1971 to 1973 as a major case where American business was able to influence a United States policy towards Africa in its favor.

The United States had supported the United Nations sanctions against Rhodesia. But after intensive lobbying by Union Carbide Corporation and Foote Mineral Company, two private United States firms with investments in Rhodesia, the American government reversed its position; and through the 1971 Byrd Amendment, the government lifted the sanctions.

Union Carbide and Foote Mineral had pushed for the lifting of the sanctions to resume the importation of chrome from Rhodesia. Rhodesia had 67.4 percent of the high grade chrome reserves in the world. In 1965, Rhodesia was the major United States source of metallurgical grade chromite, supplying 40 percent of total imports. Chromite, the third most widely used alloying material in making steel, is exceeded only by manganese and silicon. It is used primarily in the production of chrome ferro alloys, an essential ingredient in the production of stainless steel, certain alloy steels, and high temperature alloys. Chrome is also used in jet engines, aerospace, atomic energy, and also in chemicals and petrochemicals.

The sanctions meant the loss of the Rhodesian source of chromite, and American industries shifted to the Soviet Union as the major supplier. Between 1965 and 1968, the Soviet Union's share of the United States chrome imports increased from 30 percent to 60 percent. In addition to the problem of growing dependence on Russian chrome ore, there was also the problem of price increase for the ore. From a price of $30 per ton in 1966, the price of Russian ore increased to about $48 in 1969. This price increase reflected the scarcity of high quality ore partly resulting from the Rhodesian sanctions.

These facts and figures were effectively used by the anti-sanctions lobby to articulate its national security (strategic) and economic advantage arguments which, along with intensive lobbying efforts, helped the passage of the Byrd Amendment. It is important to note here that the 1971 Byrd Amendment was later repealed in 1973 through the efforts of a coalition of pro-sanctions lobby groups led by the Washington Office on Africa.

The more recent case of South African sanctions was more involved than the Rhodesian case because, in addition to the business lobby, it involved TransAfrica, the lobbying group for Africa and the Caribbean, and also the South Africa Foundation (SAF), which lobbied for the former South African government. The United States sanctions against South Africa imposed in 1986 are credited to pro-sanctions groups led by TransAfrica, which waged an aggressive campaign against the anti-sanctions groups including the South African government. The extended marches outside the South African embassy organized by TransAfrica and the arrests of political leaders and others who entered the South African embassy kept the Apartheid issue on the front burner and endeared the cause to the American people.

Support for the pro-sanctions lobby increased as more and more people came to Washington to march and express their opposition to Apartheid. This support converted to votes in Congress, and pro-sanctions groups led by TransAfrica were victorious when sanctions were imposed in 1986.

Five years later, the anti-sanctions lobby, led by the South African Foundation and the South African ambassador to Washington, staged a comeback and succeeded in having the sanctions lifted in July 1991. All the credit should not go to the ambassador and the South African Foundation. There were positive events, such as the release of Nelson Mandela and former President F.W. de Klerk's recession of some major laws of Apartheid, that contributed to softening the position of many congressmen who previously supported the sanctions.

The pro-sanctions activists attributed their defeat to being outspent by the South African lobby. The South African lobby reportedly paid more than $2 million to a dozen lobbying groups. They also ran large advertisements in magazines and newspapers beckoning American tourists to enjoy South Africa's game reserves and scenery. In the words of Ann Griffin of TransAfrica, "The South Africans are well known for their slick, behind the scenes approach here. They have sponsored trips for influential Americans, with stays in five-star hotels and tours of promising black areas, designed to show them that all is well" (*Boston Sunday Globe* July 21, 1991:4). Despite its being "slick," the South African lobbying strategy was effective in having the sanctions lifted.

ETHNIC INTEREST

When one examines the ethnic interest and the lobbying efforts of African Americans in matters pertaining to United States policies toward Africa, one finds isolated and sporadic cases of activity over the years. It was mentioned earlier that the African American leaders during the Congo crisis supported a unified Congo. This decision conformed with the stand of the majority of African leaders and was not difficult to make. In instances where African countries are divided on an issue, it becomes much harder for African Americans to decide which side to take.

A case in point would be the civil war in Nigeria that lasted from 1967 to 1970. Ogene (1983:71-72) argues that there was a lack of consensus among African Americans on the issue of whether to support the secession of Biafra or to support a united Nigeria. As a result, no united front was presented to the United States government which consequently could not weigh or take into account the views of this important sector of the American public on a major African issue.

Before the outbreak of the civil war, the American Negro Leadership Conference on Africa (ANLCA) offered its mediation to both groups to prevent the threatening disintegration. It sent a telegram to Yakubu Gowon and all the regional military governors pleading for peace and conciliation. In June 1967, the executive director of ANLCA made the first of many trips to Africa to promote a peaceful political settlement and to prepare the way for the six-man ANLCA Conciliatory Commission which never succeeded in going to Nigeria. The last projected visit was called off in March 1968 just before Martin Luther King Jr., its leader, was murdered. Part of the reason for the failure of the ANLCA mediation was the general apathy and confusion of the African American public in the United States about the crisis (Davis 242-3, cited in Ogene 1983:72).

The apathy and confusion continued until the end of the war. An interview conducted at the end of the war showed that many African Americans lacked information on and knowledge of the issues, the goals of both sides, and the area's history and personalities (*New York Times* January 14, 1970:17). As a result, many African Americans did not know what to do or say.

The lack of information or knowledge on issues pertaining to Africa was common during the 1970s, but it is no longer an excuse for African Americans not to participate in United States foreign policy making. TransAfrica, through its research and educational affiliate, TransAfrica Forum, provides useful information through *TransAfrica Forum*, a quarterly journal of opinions, and *TransAfrica News*, a news quarterly.

In addition to publishing the quarterly journal and the news quarterly, TransAfrica Forum collects, analyzes, and disseminates information about Africa, the Caribbean, and United States foreign policies affecting these regions. The forum holds annual foreign policy conferences and actively seeks to boost minority participation in United States foreign policy making through educational programs (*Black Enterprise* August 1992:58).

Hired Lobbyist as Representative of African Governments in Washington

Except for the American Israel Public Affairs Committee (AIPAC), the pro-Israel lobby that lobbies Congress explicitly for the state of Israel, there is hardly another American lobby so dedicated to the issues of a foreign country and so successful at representing them. Smith (1988:223) argues that even though AIPAC is an American lobby and not a registered foreign agent, it has close ties with the Israeli government and its tally sheets and strategy reports wind up in the Israeli Prime Minister's office. Some Israeli journalists, according to Smith, jokingly refer to AIPAC as "our embassy."

No African country or any other country for that matter has such a lobby as AIPAC. The well-meaning TransAfrica lobby focuses on the whole African continent and the Caribbean. Often, it focuses on a region such as Southern Africa or Haiti where there is a pressing human rights issue that needs to be addressed, and the lobby strives to inform and influence American policy. Like other foreign governments, African governments find that they need representation in Washington if they expect to tilt United States government decisions in their favor.

Actually, Africa has lagged behind in seeking lobbyists to represent it in Washington, partly because lobbyists are expensive and partly because African countries do not have very strong trading ties with the United States that need to be protected. Out of the countries listed by a Congressional Research Service report, as having the largest number of registered lobbying agents, six were major trading partners of the United States. They were led by Japan with 114 registered agents, Canada (81), United Kingdom (68), West Germany (53), South Korea (32), Mexico (24). Even the Soviet Union had 19 registered agents (Sachs 1991).

Lobbyists play an important role in putting issues on the front burner because they know "the ins and outs" of policy making and who the influential policy makers are. They know how to use their contacts to cut through red tape and apply direct pressure on those important to their client's interests. The stigma attached to being a lobbyist that Lipsen and Lesher (1977:3) discuss is a thing of the past. Lobbyists are no longer viewed as glorified pimps who provide members of Congress with the Three B's of politics—Booze, Broads, and Bribes.

The new breed of lobbyists are lawyers, former legislative and administrative personnel, former presidential assistants and confidants.

Recently, there has been controversy about American trade officials leaving government service to work on behalf of foreign interests. Choate (1990:50) argues that these ex-officials are highly effective in representing foreign clients because they possess a special, intimate knowledge of the inside workings of America's trade, investment, and related economic strategies. These ex-officials also have privileged access to friends, former colleagues, and former subordinates who continue to hold high government positions.

Most of the controversy has centered around Japan which hires the largest number of the ex-officials. In explaining Japan's rationale behind hiring these former officials, Choate (1990:60) writes:

> By hiring ex-officials, Japan acquires several important advantages. One of the most important is regular, unrestricted access to American leaders. Washington's network of influence...based on a fraternity of professional credentials, political appointments, and social relationships is composed primarily of former government officials who more effortlessly move between public office and private advocacy. The revolving door is their stock-in-trade: it is their livelihood.

These ex-officials do not come cheap and only rich governments with strong ties to the United States can afford to hire them on a long-term basis. Most African governments hire lobbyists for a specific short-term assignment such as lifting of sanctions or stopping Congress from cutting foreign aid to their countries. The Washington lobbying firms are more suited to these types of assignments.

Mahood (1990:58) includes among Washington's evolving lobbying establishment the "mega firm," which is a jack-of-all-trades organization offering a range of services. These lobbying services are offered to prospective clients cafeteria-style. The client chooses those services best meeting the client's needs without having to look elsewhere.

Included on the list of mega firms is Arnold and Porter; Black, Manafort, Stone, and Kelly Public Affairs Co.; Hill and Knowlton, Inc.; Ogilvy and Mather Public Affairs; the Kamber Group; and Burson-Marsteller, the New York public relations giant owned by Young and Rubicam, which in 1990 acquired Black, Manafort, Stone, and Kelly for a handsome sum, making Mr. Black and his partners multimillionaires (*The Wall Street Journal* August 14, 1992). Of the mega firms, Black, Manafort, Stone, and Kelly Public Affairs Co. has had the lion's share of lobbying for African governments.

For example, when Jonas Savimbi, the Angolan rebel leader, wanted

Washington's support for his cause, and to bring pressure on Congress and the Reagan Administration to supply him with missiles to combat Soviet tanks and jets, he engaged Black, Manafort, Stone and Kelly, the famous lobbying firm that helped elect President Bush. For $600,000 a year, beginning in 1986, this well-connected firm helped turn Savimbi, a man who collaborated with the Portuguese in the colonial era, espoused Maoist ideology, reigns despotically over troops and civilians within his territory and worked closely with white South Africa, into a "freedom fighter" fighting against communism (*Boston Globe* June 12, 1991).

The lobbying efforts of the firm were successful, and Savimbi continued to get United States aid even after the Cold War was over. In 1991 Congress voted to continue covert United States aid to the Angolan rebels after the country had concluded a superpower-brokered peace accord ending its 16-year civil war. The 1992 aid level was scaled down to about $20 million from the $60 million annual level the UNITA rebels had received through the Central Intelligence Agency (CIA) a few years earlier (*The Washington Post* June 12, 1991).

Black, Manafort, Stone, and Kelly also represents the government of Kenya which has been fighting a United States aid cut because of human rights abuses, for a fee of $6000.00 a year. The firm also gets large retainers from Nigeria (*The Wall Street Journal* August 14, 1992).

President Mobutu Sese Seko of Zaire was perhaps the most skillful African leader in influencing American policies in his favor. For many years, Mobutu used the Cold War to justify receiving millions of dollars of aid from the United States and other Western donors. These donors regarded Mobutu as a bastion against communist insurgency in the region. They continued to give him aid, despite reports of human rights abuses and suspicion that Mobutu diverted most of the aid dollars to his Swiss bank accounts.

To assure the flow of aid dollars from Washington, Mobutu engaged Black, Manafort, Stone, and Kelly. In 1989, Zaire signed a $1 million-a-year deal with the mega firm to represent it in Washington (*The Washington Post* February 19, 1990). Mobutu, however, had a good team in Washington lobbying for more aid for Zaire and making sure that the aid flow continued. The team included Tongsun Park, the influence peddler of Koreagate notoriety and veteran manipulator of United States policy makers, and Grover Connel, an international commodity merchant and one of the nation's top contributors of speaking fees to members of

Congress (*The Washington Post* March 7, 1990).

Besides having a good team working for him in Washington, Mobutu neutralized criticisms of human rights abuses by offering unsurpassed treatment to United States policy makers who visited Zaire. For example, when Representative David Dreier and three other Congressmen visited Mobutu's Versailles-like palace in Northern Zaire, they were served with wine flown in from Paris at a cost, the guests were told, of $400 a bottle. Another group of four congressmen accompanied by Mr. Connel, the international commodity merchant mentioned earlier, visited Zaire for meetings with Mobutu. All four Congressmen had been recipients of Connel Company speaking fees. While in Zaire, they were guests of the Zairian government. After their return, Rep. Robert Torricelli of New Jersey said that he came away feeling that Zaire was making "subtle" improvements in its human rights policies. Even Rep. Robert Mzarek of New York, formerly a leading Mobutu critic, toned down his criticism and sounded optimistic about events in Zaire (*The Wall Street Journal* March 7, 1990).

Mobutu's skill at influencing United States policy towards Zaire in his favor extended beyond using lobbyists. Whenever Mobutu had a chance to sway policy makers' views about Zaire, he did so by giving them royal treatment during their visits to Zaire. Such treatments won him converts such as Rep. Merryn Dymally, a California Democrat who was on the House Foreign Affairs Subcommittee on Africa. He had been a leading Mobutu defender, refusing to back the efforts of most other black congressmen to cut back on United States aid over charges of human rights abuses (*The Wall Street Journal* March 7, 1990).

It is important to note here, however, that as the Cold War ceased, the tide turned against Mobutu as the United States moved away from the Cold War criterion to stressing respect for human rights as a condition for continuing American aid. In 1990, Congress cut all military and economic aid to Mobutu's Zaire and Stipulated that $40 million in economic aid be funneled through humanitarian agencies not affiliated with the Zairian government. The Congress based its decision on charges of human rights violations and accusations that Mobutu's vast wealth was largely stolen (*The New York Times* November 4, 1990). The Congress may have felt that it was time to distance itself from the dictatorship and the cleptocracy that it had helped create in Zaire. Whereas Mobutu may have self-destructed through his acts of tyranny, his skill in influencing United States policy makers through direct and indirect lobbying will surely be emulated by other

African leaders and others around the world.

At the end of 1990, for example, the Angolan President, Jose Eduardo dos Santos, engaged the lobbyist law firm of Washington, Perito, and Dubuc to set up a two-way satellite hookup for a face-to-face meeting between the Angolan President in his faraway capital, Luanda, and 18 members of Congress in the Rayburn Building. Dos Santos wanted to lay out his case against America's controversial covert aid program to rebels in that country.

Lawyer Robert B. Washington, Jr. travelled to Angola to brief dos Santos on everything from policy to what to wear on television. The resultant chat between the Angolan President and the Congressmen was quite impressive. The cost to the Angola government was $75,000 (*The Washington Post* September 17, 1990).

It is possible that for African governments, the trend in the future will be an increased use of Washington lobby firms to cut through red tape and get their issues to United States policy makers in the shortest time period possible. These governments, however, must have a clear goal of what they want to accomplish. The goals must be realistic, and they should not expect lobbyists to perform miracles. Nor should these governments waste money on meaningless ceremonial gestures.

A case in point would be a 1989 United States visit by the Somali Prime Minister, Gen. Muhammad Ali Samantar, who wanted an audience with President Bush. Somalia hired Black, Manafort, Stone, and Kelly to arrange the meeting. The firm was able to arrange an appointment for Samantar with Vice President Danforth Quayle. The Vice President's busy schedule, however, had room only for a stand-up handshake and a photo with Samantar and nothing more. But to Quayle's obvious surprise, Samantar sat, expecting to chat. Quayle kept the meeting short, and the incident proved embarrassing for Samantar and the lobby firm (*The Washington Post* February 19, 1990).

The obvious question that comes to mind about this incident is the following: Did the Somali head of state know that he was paying thousands of dollars for a photo opportunity with Vice President Quayle? Perhaps not! And obviously a small, poor country like Somalia cannot afford to pay thousands of dollars to a Washington consultant simply to get a picture of its head of state taken with the United States President or the Vice President.

Conclusion

It is important to emphasize that a country knows what services it seeks to buy from lobbyists. If, for example, the country needs an hour's audience with the United States President to discuss a given problem, then, the client country's desire must be conveyed to the lobbyist in no uncertain terms and assurances sought that the hour would be available.

There are laws governing the activities of lobbyists in Washington, and African governments need to acquaint themselves with these laws as they increase their demand for the services of these lobbyists. Needless to say, an increase in demand for lobbyists by these countries and other countries including the newly democratized former eastern block countries would raise the fees charged by the lobbyists unless the increase is matched by an increase in the number of new lobbyists. The steep fees would shut out many African countries. These countries would be forced to turn to non-profit lobby groups such as TransAfrica if they want lobbyist representation. Such an increase in demand for TransAfrica lobbying services would place an enormous burden on the meager resources of the group.

Actually, the needs of African countries when regional conflicts are excluded are not that diverse and can be represented by one powerful United States lobby. TransAfrica has played a key role in informing and influencing American policies on some of the more pressing issues such as Apartheid in South Africa. The resources of the lobby group are, however, too meager to take on the task of representing the demands of some 50 African countries adequately.

Chapter Four
United States Economic Assistance to Africa

Abdul Karim Bangura

INTRODUCTION

The United States economic assistance program examined in this chapter includes the bilateral development aid and economic support funding from 1980 to 1992 geared toward helping the citizens of the following countries in Sub-Saharan Africa which received the assistance: Benin, Botswana, Burkina Fasso (formerly Upper Volta), Burundi, Cameroon, Cape Verde, Central African Republic, Chad, Congo, Djibouti, Equatorial Guinea, Gambia, Ghana, Guinea, Guinea-Bissau, Kenya, Lesotho, Liberia, Malawi, Mali, Mauritania, Mauritius, Niger, Rwanda, Sao Tome and Principe, Senegal, Seychelles, Sierra Leone, Somalia, Sudan, Swaziland, Tanzania, Togo, Uganda, Zaire, Zambia, and Zimbabwe. Administered by the United States Agency for International Development (USAID), the American economic assistance program for these countries was funded through capital transfers and technical assistance.

As the data for United States development assistance to various USAID-classified geopolitical regions from 1980 to 1992, summarized in Table 1, reveal, Africa's share of the total aid ranged between twenty-six to forty percent from 1980 to 1988. In 1989 and 1990, Africa received two percent and one percent of the total aid, respectively. USAID estimated share of the aid for the continent was only one percent of the total aid in 1991; the agency's requested amount (from Congress) for the continent in 1992 was also one percent of the total aid.

The dramatic decline in United States economic assistance to Sub-Saharan Africa came at a time when countries in that region were facing (and continue to face) some of the most difficult economic and political problems. This was at a time when out of the forty-six poorest countries in the world, thirty one were in Sub-Saharan Africa.

The decline hinged on two major reasons. The first had to do with the fact that the Reagan and Bush Administrations gave a higher priority to providing military and security-related assistance rather than economic aid to African states. During these administrations, government requests for foreign military sales credits climbed by over 300 percent. During this same period, the level of security-related assistance climbed 200 percent (Trans-Africa 1982). As Kimaru points out in chapter three of this book, Kenya, Somalia, Sudan, and Zaire received the bulk of this aid partly because of their effective lobbying efforts.

The second reason is that United States assistance was perceived to have strategic interests. Thus, the bulk of the American aid went to regions where the United States felt that its political and economic interests could be effectively pursued, not necessarily to the poorest and neediest regions of the world.

Table 1. United States Bilateral Development Assistance to Various Geopolitical Regions, 1980–1992 (in $ millions)

Year	Africa		Latin America and the Caribbean		*Asia*		*Near East*		Asia and Near East		Europe & Near East	
	$	%	$	%	$	%	$	%	$	%	$	%
1980	268	28	257	27	392	41	34	4	—	—	—	—
1981	300	30	233	24	397	40	61	6	—	—	—	—
1982	329	31	280	27	400	38	39	4	—	—	—	—
1983	315	29	329	30	392	36	44	5	—	—	—	—
1984	340	32	295	27	—	—	—	—	444	41	—	—
1985	352	26	507	37	—	—	—	—	494	37	—	—
1986	379	30	462	36	—	—	—	—	442	34	—	—
1987	397	31	437	35	—	—	—	—	428	34	—	—
1988	544	40	416	31	—	—	—	—	389	29	—	—

Table 1 continued on next page.

1989	99	2	462	14	15	1	–	–	–	–	2,801	83
1990	29	1	1,094	27	13	1	–	–	–	–	2,867	71
1991	33	1	713	21	20	1	–	–	–	–	2,599	77
1992	28	1	714	22	18	1	–	–	–	–	2,468	76

Note: The 1980-1990 data are actually disbursed amounts; the 1991 data are estimated amounts; the 1992 data are requested amounts; amounts for 1989-1992 are rounded off to the nearest million. Source: USAID, *Congressional Presentations, Fiscal Years 1983-1990, Main Volumes.* Washington, DC: (USAID Publications) Government Printing Office.

Meanwhile, the poor countries got poorer. States which were perceived to be clients of the Soviet Union were eliminated from the program or got drastically cut. The Reagan and Bush Administrations refused to provide economic assistance to Mozambique or to send an American Ambassador to that country. The American aid program in Ethiopia was closed, and the United States had no Ambassador there. In addition, no formal diplomatic relations were established between the United States and Angola.

In order to delineate those factors that might have led to the preceding developments, at least four major questions can be posed: (1) What political perspectives and traditions shape the way Americans look at African and other developing countries? (2) What are the purposes of American foreign assistance to African and other developing countries? (3) How is United States foreign aid policies toward Africa shaped? (4) What type of foreign aid doctrine did the Reagan and Bush Administrations espouse from 1980 to 1992 (the period of the major focus in this book)? The sections below explore these questions.

AMERICAN POLITICAL PERSPECTIVES AND TRADITIONS

The following words from May are quite apt in describing what drive American policy makers as they design United States foreign aid policies toward Africa:

> Framers of foreign policy are often influenced by beliefs about what history teaches or portends. Sometimes, they perceive problems in terms of analogies from the past. Sometimes, they envision the future either as foreshadowed by historical parallels or as following a straight line from what has recently gone before (1973:ix).

Sewell and Mathieson (1982:5-8) suggest four factors—abundance, individualism and democracy, revolution and social change, economic liberalism and attitudes toward poverty—that shape the ways in which Americans look at Africa with other developing countries and their development. They add that these four factors are, in turn, shaped by the attitudes and values rooted in the American political system and institutions. The following discussion on the four factors is based mostly on Sewell and Mathieson's essay and a few other works.

Abundance

The political and economic traditions that are today prevalent in the United States were shaped by settlers on a continent with enormous space, rich natural resources, sparse population, and no rigid social structure. This combination encouraged individual initiative. As long as existing assets were limitless and differences over the redistribution of wealth rarely arose, there was little need to confront the difficult choice of how to divide the riches (Sewell and Mathieson 1982:5).

As a result, American social development continually began over and again on the frontier. This perennial rebirth, this fluidity of American life, this expansion westward with its new opportunities, its continuous touch with the simplicity of primitive society, unleashed the forces that dominated the American character (Turner 1963:28).

Given their national experience of relative physical abundance and few political and social control, American citizens tend to assume that change and development are relatively easy. Consequently, the lack of initiative is frequently seen as the culprit when economic progress does not take place at home or in developing countries. Very little blame is seldom accorded determinants such as scarce national resources or inadequate social structures (Sewell and Mathieson 1982:5).

Individualism and Democracy

The United States escaped a rigid class structure mainly because the European immigrants and their descendants who shaped the nation's socio-economic structure had fled economic calamities, oppressive governments, and restrictive class structures. Thus, the individual emerged as the cornerstone of the American social and economic order. Individual rights and participation, therefore, became the foundation of America's political democracy. This tenet propels the United States to check sometimes arbitrary central governments in developing countries (Sewell and

Mathieson 1982:5-6). On certain occasions, however, the American government ignores calls by opponents of ruthless central governments which are strong allies of the United States. A case in point was Mobutu's government in Zaire.

A contemporary American president who championed the notion of individualism and democracy in United States foreign policy is Ronald Reagan. When Reagan first ran for the presidency, the global economy was in a serious recession. Reagan took office questioning the assumptions that undergirded economic assistance from the Western industrialized countries to the developing countries of Africa. The global economic recession offered Reagan the opportunity to proselytize the blessings of the free market system. He sought to release the energies of the free market on the American economy. Reagan promised to "get the government off the backs of hard-working Americans" to allow them to reap the full benefits of their labor with as few government regulations as possible. In time, he tried to sell this cause to the rest of the world (Khapoya 1994:293).

Revolution and Social Change
Even though Americans like to think of their country as a former colony, a state created by revolution, this revolution was of a different sort, however. The American revolution was neither radical nor ideological. Instead, it was a "practical" revolution that sought self-determination (Sewell and Mathieson 1982:6).

Americans generally look at revolutions, such as the one that took place in Cuba under Fidel Castro, as bad. They believe that the costs of violent social upheaval outweigh the gains. This notion hinges on the idea that moderate reformist solutions to political conflict are healthy for economic prosperity (Sewell and Mathieson 1982:6).

It is no surprise, therefore, that the United States observed the passing of colonialism in Africa with a mix of approval and apprehension. On the one hand, the American heritage was anticolonial; the national instinct was to applaud Africa's advance from European colonial rule to self-government. On the other hand, the fact that African nationalism emerged during the cold war made the United States apprehensive about the challenge to the hegemony of the Western alliance on the continent. Rather than wholeheartedly support independence movements throughout Africa, American policy leaned towards damage limitation. When the Congo crisis erupted in 1960, the Eisenhower Administration feared major damage to Western interests. Much of United States policy towards Africa since then, according to some observers, has been influenced by the "Congo syndrome": the fear of radical nationalism in Africa (Chazan et al 1988:372-373).

Economic Liberalism and Attitudes toward Poverty

Classical liberal economic thought remains strong in the United States mainly because Americans believe that the market mechanism should not be impeded, although occasional government interventions are welcomed. Consequently, large segments of the American public are against most forms of government regulation and planning (Sewell and Mathieson 1982:6).

This preference for economic liberalism and free-market economies make American government officials reluctant to discuss proposals for a New International Economic Order (NIEO). While the facilitating of equality of opportunity is considered a praiseworthy objective, any attempt to level incomes, however, is seen as a fruitless and needless endeavor. Thus, Americans are never enthusiastic about calls for tackling income inequalities either within a country or between countries. American support for basic human needs programs in developing countries and opposition to proposals for a NIEO are consistent, therefore, with its deep seated belief of economic liberalism (Sewell and Mathieson 1982:7).

One of the earliest post-colonial links between the United States and African nationalism came in the area of American education. This link was bolstered by John F. Kennedy on the eve of his election. Kenya's Tom Mboya saw Kennedy in 1960 in connection with attempts to raise money for 260 Kenyan students who had been admitted into a number of American colleges but did not have the money for fares. Kennedy took up the matter with the Kennedy Foundation, and a $100,000 grant was provided (Mazrui 1977:156).

As soon as he took office, Kennedy appealed to the missionary strain in the American temperament. He said to his fellow Americans:

> Since this country was founded, each generation of Americans has been summoned to give testimony to its national loyalty....Now the trumpet summons us again—not as a call to bear arms, though arms we need—not as a call to battle, though embattled we are—but a call to bear the burden of a long twilight struggle, year in year out, 'rejoicing in hope, patient tribulation'—a struggle against the common enemies of man: tyranny, poverty, disease and war itself (Mazrui 1977:156-157).

However, the missionary factor in the American temperament is not without its dangers. Sometimes it takes the form of an ideological crusade. American anti-communism, for example, is akin to the doctrine of 'manifest destiny'—the combination of missionary zeal and patriotism that creates a militancy that is both outward-looking and self-centered (Mazrui 1977:157).

Kennedy attempted to isolate the boy scout from the ideological crusader within the American missionary when he stated the following in his inaugural address:

> To those peoples in the huts and villages of half the globe struggling to break the bonds of mass misery, we pledge our best efforts to help them help themselves, for whatever period is required—not because the Communists may be doing it, not because we seek their votes, but because it is right (Mazrui 1977:157).

Indeed, Kennedy's inaugural address was an approximation to real intention. But a complete separation of the boy scout from the ideological crusader was an overly ambitious goal. Kennedy brought a new emphasis on the boy scout side, but his Peace Corps and, even more clearly, his Alliance for Progress could not be completely separated from motives of ideological proselytism (Mazrui 1977:157).

THE PURPOSES OF AMERICAN FOREIGN AID

In examining the debate over the purposes of American foreign assistance to Africa and other developing countries, one is able to discern at least two major contending schools of thought. These are the *classical* and the *critical*.

Classical School

Proponents of the classical school see American foreign aid as important if used appropriately: that is, if it can contribute to break bottlenecks (massive poverty, illiteracy, low life expectancy, malnutrition, unemployment, etc.) in development and encourage innovation. This presupposition, Hettne (1978:44-45) suggests, is a "missionary assumption" that the United States and other Western countries are going to save the world—the idea of nature as an object to be mastered and exploited. This thinking is generally ingrained in the United States development aid policy. As an annual report of President Gerald Ford transmitted to Congress in May 1975, for example, boldly asserts:

> Over the past decade, the economies of the developing countries have grown at an encouraging rate. This was particularly because of American assistance. Consequently, many nations no longer need assistance on the concessional terms we once extended (USDCC 1975:i).

This school of thought can be traced to the "Western" model of development. In the words of Nisbet (1969:7), "developmentalism is one of the oldest and most powerful of all Western ideas." The central idea of this development thinking is the metaphor of growth. Thus development, according to Nisbet, is conceived as being "organic, immanent, directional, cumulative, irreversible, and purposive. Furthermore, it implies structural differentiation and increasing complexity." Certainly, the emphasis within this perspective has shifted and new elements have been introduced during the history of Western civilization. The emergence of capitalism and the bourgeoisie as the dominant class must have given a certain shape to Western developmentalism. This is one reason why some observers have branded the intellectual movements in 17th century Europe as the birthplace of Western development thinking. The successes of the Marshall Plan[1] in Europe helped to set the stage for the early discussion of modern economic development.

The discussion of modern economic development (that is, the 1950s and the early 1960s) had an optimistic tone which cannot be explained today. This optimism hinged on two factors: (1) the dynamic economic growth experienced by the industrialized countries themselves under the Marshall Plan as a successful demonstration case in development and (2) the philosophic tradition in the West which looked upon growth as more or less inevitable. The Keynesian "revolution" in economics had taught Western economists that the state sometimes had to give a helping hand, but few doubted that the future of developing countries on the whole was reflected in the experience of the industrialized countries. The simple formula was the following: just find out the Incremental Capital-Output ratio and the desired rate of growth. Then one can (after due consideration to the rate of population growth) arrive at the appropriate level of investment needed for economic growth. Foreign capital inflows were seen as a 'pump-priming' mechanism intended to help a recipient country's savings and tax receipts as well as investment to rise steadily (for details, see MacBean and Balasubramanyam 1976:147-148).

More sociologically-minded authors also stressed the importance of a leading sector (private or public) and the emergence of an entrepreneurial elite as stimuli for economic development. Growth, as expounded by scholars such as Rostow (1960), was thus seen mainly as a function of investment and not too many observers doubted that a process of economic growth through a series of "stages" would in the end benefit an entire country. This is why the 1960s were heralded the First Development Decade in anticipation of what was expected to follow.

During the early 1970s, however, many African and other developing countries began to encounter difficulties in fulfilling this development strategy. Even those economists trained in formal theory began to sense new realities. Adelman and Morris, for example, capture this idea quite well when they state the following:

> We had shared the prevailing view among economists that economic growth was economically beneficial to most nations. We had also greatly questioned the relevance today of the historical association of successful economic growth with the spread of parliamentary democracy. Our results proved to be at variance with our preconceptions (1973:vii).

It is evident from this excerpt that these scholars exemplify a renewed interest in the connection between economic growth and income distribution. One reason for this emphasis was the visible aspects of the extent of poverty: recurrent starvation, mass unemployment, political unrest, etc. What was taking place in many African and other developing countries during the 'development decade' was growth with poverty, instead of development.

As the special issue report on "Poverty and Inequality" in *World Development* (1978) reveals, poverty is in fact enormously multidimensional. It may, therefore, be questioned if one can actually get a better insight into this problem with the aid of ordinary income analysis, since poverty could also be identified with reference to social and economic classes, rural and urban residence, regions, ethnic groups, etc. A distinction should also be made between poverty on the one hand and political inequality on the other. Policies directed toward the elimination of poverty may not necessarily be the same policies aimed at reducing inequality. Whereas the former are concerned with irreducible and minimal issues, the latter must go deeper into the structured patterns of access to wealth, knowledge, and decision-making institutions. The former can be included in conventional growth models (redistribution with growth) and the latter policies are of qualitatively different types.

There are, however, those who have also argued that poverty should be structurally defined if the underlying causes of poverty are to be removed. Proponents of this view include Griffin and Kahn (1978). On this level, policies of poverty elimination and policies of inequality reduction converge. This is where the main divide between different schools of how to eradicate poverty can be found.

The new strategy implied in the "redistribution with growth" discussion exemplified a modification of, rather than a clear break with, previous strategies. First, the analysis retained much of the optimism of the earlier "trickle down" models in asserting that the benefits of growth, empirically, had a tendency to be concentrated in the early stages but that further increases in concentration were by no means inevitable. Secondly, the social engineering approach to development, as Chenery and his partners (1962, 1963, 1966a, 1966b) purported, was still adhered to, in that they believed that to deal with the problems of poverty groups governments need to design overall programs or policy packages rather than a set of isolated projects. This is simply a continuation of the old approach of "balanced growth" extended to include social development as well.

The rather dismal post-war record (up to the 1970s) of development plans propelled the Institute of Development Studies (in Sussex, England) to bring together a large number of experts to probe the difficult questions raised by the planning experience (Faber and Seers 1972). As emphasized by Seers (1972:21) in a contribution to this work, a plan has to take account of the government's economic and political aims, and politicians are busy people: "They have to keep an eye on the parliamentary situation and on the balance-of-power within the cabinet, not to speak of pondering rumors of invasion or threats of assassination." Intellectuals, on the other hand, are more concerned with reaching a "correct" decision from a logical or theoretical perspective. After that, they usually lose interest.

Occasionally, as Hettne (1978:25) points out, politicians are intellectuals. Julius Nyerere of Tanzania, for example, was extremely interested in planning and implemented his Ujamaa (socialist) villages program.[2] By 1975, Nyerere and his government had largely backed down from the idea of communal production.

Such difficulties led Leys (1977:56) to suggest that planning is to be thought of in terms that required the world to be other than it is, if planning is to work. This type of situation, still according to Leys, may be said to mark the end of the dominance of a certain paradigm and initiate a heterodox search for another. This search led to the critical school of thought.

Critical School
This school sees the whole complex of American and other development aid, in many respects, to be a typical example of quasi-reform. The functions of American and other aid are perceived to be many: to make "weak" economies capable of joining the international capitalist market, to make them more able to suppress internal rebellions, to link them to one or the other of the main political blocs, and to facilitate the spread of the Western model of development (Hettne 1978:25).

This school emerged as a cry for a marxist and non-marxist alternative to the classical school. The call for the "indigenization" of social sciences, particularly development theory, in developing countries is further development of this thought. This was an outcome of the confrontation between "Western" concepts and theories on the one hand and the social reality in developing countries on the other. Obviously, the intensity of this confrontation has varied from country to country, mainly depending on the extent of Western intellectual penetration. (The efforts at indigenization of development thinking are treated in this chapter as a process of political and economic emancipation.) The theories that have developed in the developing countries ("New International Economic Order," "dependencia," "self-reliance," and "indigenization") have dealt with imperialism as a Western problem connected with the accumulation process in mature capitalism. These theories have provided an antithesis and a healthy corrective, stating that Asia and Africa contained within them legacies of European colonial systems (and by implication, American neo-colonialism) that continue to retard their development processes (Hodgkin 1972:106).

However, going through the more recent literature on development and underdevelopment (that is, from the early 1970s to the mid-1980s), one is struck by the fact that there is one paradigm which dominated a large number of analyses, namely what has been referred to as the "dependence paradigm." The dependence paradigm, according to a common view, emerged as a result of the merger of two intellectual trends, one can be referred to as (following Foster-Carter 1974, 1976) neo-marxism, the other rooted in the Latin American discussion on development. As to "neo-marxism," this concept has been suggested to account for a certain dualism in marxist thinking: that is, on the one hand, the traditional approach focusing on the concept of development and taking a basically eurocentric view, and, on the other hand, a more recent approach (neo-marxism), focusing on the concept of underdevelopment and expressing a developing world view. Consequently, a lot of controversy has arisen as to the continuity or discontinuity in these two approaches.

The second important background to the breakthrough of the dependence paradigm in development theory has been the Latin American "dependencia" school, rooted in specific economic and intellectual experiences of Latin American countries, particularly during the depression of the 1930s. A development strategy emphasizing "desarrollo hacia adentro" (inward looking development) was made popular by the United Nations Economic Commission for Latin America (ECLA) with headquarters in Santiago de Chile from 1948. The main theme that was put forward by the ECLA-team of economists was that economic theory as expounded in developed capitalist countries was inadequate and there was a need for more structural approaches, including an appreciation of different historical situations and national contexts (O'Brien 1975:9). The remedy on the level of economic policy was thought to be industrialization based on import-substitution. A number of observers have demonstrated that this strategy was, if not wrong, at least inadequate (see especially World Development 1977:1-2).

This situation provided the incentive for the elaboration and extension of the dependency approach resulting in a variety of dependency schools. Some of these views were continuations of the old ECLA-strategy, others oriented toward marxism.

These ideas, which so clearly emerged from the empirical reality of Latin America (and the Caribbean region), constituted the most formidable challenge that the eurocentric concepts and theories of development had faced so far. They had a strong impact on Western scholars working in the area (notably Andre Gunder Frank 1979) and, thus formulated, they began to conquer the Western academic community from the late 1960s to the 1980s. In this way, two conflicting paradigms in development theory arose.

That the two schools of development theory ("from tradition to modernity" and "dependence to underdevelopment") constitute competing and incompatible paradigms can be seen in the obvious lack of communication between them. This is taken to be an important criterion of paradigmatic shift (in Thomas Kuhn's usage). As suggested by Foster-Carter and Hettne, this problem of communication gap could be studied in the editorial policies of various journals. The new paradigm (dependency) has been reflected in the contributions of journals such as *Journal for Contemporary Asia, Review of African Political Economy*, and of course, *Monthly Review*. Gradually, it received a kind of mainstream legitimacy by getting a fairly generous treatment in such regular development journals as *World Development, Journal of Development Studies* and *Journal of Peace Research*. Somewhat surprisingly, one article by Dos Santos (1970) can be found in the *American Economic Review*, but this appears to be an exceptional case. Dependence was never able to conquer the stronghold of the old paradigm: *Economic Development and Cultural Change*.

Following the proposition of the classical school, then, an empirical analysis of the effects of American foreign aid to Africa should find that, as the level of United States development assistance increases to those countries, so would overall economic development in those countries. But in light of the position of the critical school, such an empirical study should find that increases in American development assistance to African countries would lead to negative economic effects in those countries. Unfortunately, the required quantitative exercise to test these propositions is beyond the scope of this chapter.

THE SHAPING OF UNITED STATES FOREIGN AID POLICIES TOWARD AFRICA

In order to examine those aspects that shape United States foreign aid policies toward Africa, the following conceptual framework is suggested:

Figure 1. The Making of United States Foreign Aid Policies Toward Africa

Political and Strategic Interests	Economic Interests	The Political Process	Type & Level of United States Foreign Aid to Africa
A. United States Expansionism	A. Trade	A. Executive Branch	
B. Retrenchment	B. Commodities	B. Congress	
	C. Energy	C. Budget Process	
	D. International Investments	D. Interest Groups	
		E. Minority and Ethnic Groups	
F E E D B A C K			

Political and Strategic Interests

American political and strategic interests in Africa, in a general sense, are a reflection of the global interests that have shaped United States foreign policy since World War II. As Sewell and Mathieson (1982:9) suggest, although these objectives are shared by the overwhelming majority of the American population, numerous differences of opinion emerge as to their relative merits and the best way to achieve them. What is frequently not clear is whether or not it is in the best interest of the United States to aid dictatorial allies, such as Mobutu, with arms and funds which they use to suppress their people.

It is quite obvious that the pursuit of any goal can be a taxing exercise for any country, even the United States. It is equally obvious that United States relations with African countries were less predictable compared to those of, say, Western Europe, simply because of the belief that no serious communist threat was perceived in Africa. However, as Hill points out in chapter five of this book, there were certain African countries that were perceived by the United States to be "stooges" of the former communist bloc, and therefore, received a reasonable degree of attention in Washington: Libya, Egypt (under President Gamal Abdel Nasser), Angola, Mozambique, and Ethiopia.

While no African country threatens the sanctity of American borders in a military sense, the United States has historically viewed the security and stability of major sea-lanes (the Suez Canal, Cape Horn, the Cape of Good Hope); and other mineral-rich and strategically located countries such as Zaire, Sudan, Kenya, Egypt, Somalia, South Africa, Namibia, Morocco, and Nigeria as important to its international and economic stability.

United States Expansionism. Discounting the period of slavery, the United States first became actively involved in Africa in the late 19th and early 20th centuries when America emerged from relative isolation and began acting as a global power, intervening in the affairs of other countries when it suited its interests. There are many reasons for the shift from isolationism to expansionism. Sewell and Mathieson (1982:10-11) suggest the following: (a) a desire to emulate the Europeans, who had colonized Africa and Asia; (b) the end of the seemingly limitless open frontier; (c) the transformation of the American economy from agriculture to manufacturing; (d) the increasing acceptance of Darwin's theory of evolution with its supposedly biological evidence of Anglo-Saxon supremacy; (e) the growing concept that sea power was essential for world power, which prompted the United States to build a large modern navy.

In almost the same manner that the United States evoked the Monroe Doctrine to plant its flag in the Caribbean, Latin American, Hawaii, Puerto Rico, Cuba, to name a few, the United States also forcibly moved residents from Cabo Delgado (an island off the coast of Southern Africa) to the Comoro Islands in its efforts to monitor the naval fleets of the Soviet Union in vital sea-lanes of the Pacific Ocean. The residents of those islands were in no position to oppose American military forces.

Retrenchment. United States strategic thinking about African countries began to change in the late 1960s, influenced strongly by the unrest at home and the humiliation in Vietnam. The emphasis shifted from the direct use of United States troops to an increased reliance on friendly governments and local forces. This new policy had a corollary: the United States would continue to supply arms, equipment, and other forms of support necessary to help its African allies counter external aggression or internal subversions led or inspired by the Soviet Union or China.

As Volman (1980:4) points out, between 1973 and 1978, the volume of arms transfers to Africa increased tenfold, from $300 million to over $3 billion annually, making Africa the second largest arms market in the developing world (the largest being the Middle East). Most of the arms received by African countries came from three major sources: the Soviet Union, France, and the United States. The Soviet Union provided about 50 percent of the arms, France about 25 percent, and the United States about 13 percent. The remaining 12 percent was supplied by several European producers (Great Britain, West Germany, Italy, Switzerland, and Sweden), by the People's Republic of China, and by two developing world arms producers (Israel and Brazil).

As stated earlier, the Reagan and Bush Administrations gave a higher priority to providing military and security-related assistance rather than economic aid to African countries. This was at a time when there was a sharp decline in overall development aid to the continent, and its economic and political woes were mounting.

Economic Interests

As stated earlier, before 1960 United States economic activities in Africa were relatively insignificant (if we discount the Atlantic slave trade, of course). As the United States economy matured, American businesses became more active on the continent.

Trade. Following years of rapid expansion, United States exports to Africa abruptly reversed their high growth pace in the first half of 1982. Shipments were off eight percent in the first six months of 1982, and the total American exports to Sub-Saharan Africa fell below the $6 billion mark (United States Department of Commerce 1982:22). Many factors were responsible for this reversal.

One was the fact that Africa was in an economic crisis. Continued stagnation in export earnings, high rates of population growth, and mounting burdens of international debts plagued many countries on the continent. In some cases, these problems were exacerbated by poor policy decisions.

Furthermore, most African countries are monocrop or single-mineral economies. Because of the economic reorganization in the developed countries in the 1980s (due to recession, unemployment, stagnation, and economic uncertainties), some African countries could not find suitable outlets for their goods.

Nigeria and South Africa, which together account for about two-thirds of United States sales to Africa in a normal year, were suffering the effects of soft world markets for oil and minerals. In Nigeria, the world-wide oil glut of 1981-1982 caused a drastic shortfall in export revenue. Oil sales to the United States, Nigeria's leading customer, were off by nearly 40 percent in the first five months of 1982 alone. South Africa's export earnings experienced a similar decline due mainly to the drop in the price of gold (United States Department of Commerce 1982:22). Both countries (Nigeria and South Africa), therefore, took firm steps to restrict their imports in order to protect their balance of payments.

Also, United States exports to Africa declined because of the strong dollar. The dollar appreciated nearly 15 percent against the Special Drawing Right (SDR) between April 1980 and April 1982, cutting deeply into United States export competitiveness world-wide, and especially in the capital-scarce markets of Africa. The strong dollar also cut into the profits oil-exporting African countries would have gained from the falling oil prices (United States Department of Commerce 1982:22).

Commodities. In spite of the economic problems Africa faces, the United States continues to be dependent on the continent's minerals. And as Jackson (1982:169-170) suggests, the Arab oil boycott of 1973-1974 demonstrated the usefulness of a vital natural resource as a weapon of political policy among the developing world producers. African minerals have become similarly essential to the American economy and have established their role in the future of America as the sole super power. Certain minerals are concentrated in only a few regions of the world. Southern Africa, for example, has 86 percent of the world reserves of platinum group metals, 53 percent of manganese, 52 percent of cobalt, 64 percent of vanadium, and 95 percent of the world's reserves of chromium. It comes as no surprise, thus, that the United States supported the racist government in South Africa for many years (see Dumbuya's discussion of the role of minerals in American-South African relations in chapter two).

Jackson also notes that American vulnerability in minerals has become as acute as its oil dependency in many respects. The point is underscored in the Santini Congressional Report, which concludes that "no issue facing America in the decades ahead poses the risks and dangers to the national economy and defense as United States dependency on foreign sources for strategic and critical minerals" (Jackson 1982:182-183). The American Society of Metals iterates this view when it suggests the following: "A cutoff of our chromium supply could be even more serious than a cutoff of our oil supply. We do have some oil but we have almost no chromium" (Jackson 1982:183).

C. Energy. Since United States consumption of energy is higher than what it produces, it seeks sufficient supply of energy at predictable prices (which is not necessarily the same as low or unchanging prices) for adequate but prudent use of industries and individuals. But historically, United States consumption has been less than prudent. Decades of abundance and declining real prices led to wasteful consumption. In 1979, for example, per capita consumption of energy in the United States, about 12,350 kilograms of coal equivalent, was more than 56 percent higher than the average consumption of industrialized countries (7,892 kilograms), and nearly 100 times that for low-income countries other than China and India (129 kilograms). The reduced supply of oil and price rises of the 1970s altered the pattern (Sewell and Mathieson 1982:28).

For Africa, Nigeria emerged as one of the richest countries in the world in terms of natural resources in the 1970s and the 1980s, and oil represented the key to its new wealth. Concomitant with this wealth came an emergent position of political leverage vis-a-vis the United States and other industrialized countries.

Nigerian petroleum producers in 1980 averaged a daily yield of 2.2 million barrels of the country's crude. It was priced by Americans because of its high-quality, low-sulfur oil that can yield more gasoline per barrel than the heavier Middle Eastern crude. American importers bought a million barrels, or almost half of the production, every day. United States imports of Nigerian oil grew so rapidly in the decade between 1970 (when the United States imported none) and 1980 (when Nigeria provided as much as 16 percent of American oil import) that Nigeria emerged as a creditor to the United States (Jackson 1982:171).

International Investments. United States investments in Africa are highly visible and important to both host and sending countries. Despite the fact that these investments further the 'dependency' of African countries upon the United States (for reasons suggested earlier), it is obvious, however, that the investments do provide the host countries with capital and technology needed to create some jobs. But clearly, South Africa has emerged the biggest winner of American investments in Africa.

The increased level of United States investments in South Africa are a substantial benefit to United States economic interests. The favorable balance of trade is particularly important in view of the continuing United States deficits in its international balance of payments and its troubles with economic recession at home. The favorable terms are attractive too: largely because of cheap African labor, the annual rate of return on direct American investments in South Africa, for instance, ranged from 17 percent in 1968 to 19 percent in 1976 (El-Khawas and Cohen 1976:28).

The differing trade needs of the two counties are also compatible. The United States sells industrial goods to South Africa that significantly benefit South Africa's economic expansion in such areas as computer technology, heavy-capital goods, oil exploration, and chemical industries. In return, the United States imports crucial minerals, such as platinum, chromium, and gold from South Africa. All these activities by the United States did help to perpetuate the racist South African system for a long time, since South Africa viewed them as partial approval of its social, economic, and political systems.

The Political Process

Executive Branch. It need not be belabored here that the Executive branch of the American Federal government has no centralized structure for making decisions or implementing policy on the broad range of issues that concern African countries. Functional areas of responsibility are widely dispersed among federal departments and agencies, each of which jealously guards its independence and influence. Interdepartmental rivalries and conflicts are inevitable and often result in fundamental policies.

For example, as Sewell and Mathieson (1982:28) note, the State Department oversees relations with individual governments in African countries. As a group, it assigns them a lower priority than either the industrialized countries or Russia and its former allies. The State Department maintains control over bilateral development assistance through the United States Agency for International Development (USAID). Because economic development is only one of the State Department's foreign policy concerns, it often views development assistance as primarily a political instrument, a view which at times has caused major conflicts within USAID.

With authority so diffused, the role of the individual USAID policy maker often becomes exceedingly crucial. Who does and does not dominate the bureaucracy varies from time to time and from administration to administration.

Congress. Congress plays a role in determining foreign policy that is perhaps unique among the industrial countries. It shares authority over foreign policy—including power over war, treaties, appointments, and commerce—with the Executive branch. In addition, Congress has effective control over budgetary authorizations and appropriations (fondly referred to as "the power of the purse"), including foreign aid expenditures. This wide rage of powers makes it possible for Congress to negate Executive branch initiatives if it so wishes or, alternatively, to put forward its own programs. Power is, however, more dispersed within Congress than within the Executive branch. For example, 13 of 19 standing committees have some responsibility for foreign economic expenditures and legislation, and almost 50 sub-committees have some jurisdiction over issues significantly affecting African countries.

However, Congress' recent record in foreign affairs is mixed. The Executive branch maintains that legislators have been mainly obstructive. Congress claims that on some issues, particularly in the area of international development policy, it has taken a constructive lead. It was Congress, not the Executive branch, that initiated the reforms of the American foreign aid program to focus on basic human needs in 1973 (Sewell and Mathieson 1982:31).

Budgetary Process. Decision making within the American government is closely tied to the process of formulating, authorizing, and appropriating the annual federal budget. The budget itself has become the main vehicle for determining federal defense and domestic social policy. The process works well, except for those areas of public policy that are not large budgetary items. Although foreign aid, for example, is only a small part of the overall transactions between the United States and African countries, the annual foreign aid legislation tends to dominate discussions of policies toward those countries. As the aid bill goes through the legislative process, it consumes an inordinate amount of time and attention of both the Executive branch and Congress (Sewell and Mathieson 1982:32).

Interest Groups. A variety of organized groups affect American policies toward African countries. Trade unions, for example, which generally have played a leadership role in social reform efforts in the United States, remain a potent political force despite the fact that the overall rate of unionization of the labor force has declined. However, many unions in recent years have hardened their outlook on relations with developing countries for reasons of both self-interest and altered domestic economic conditions.

Until the mid-1960s, when the United States still enjoyed a monopoly in the manufacture of capital- and technology-intensive products, the trade unions favored free trade and open markets. As the trade balance swung into deficit and the United States' manufacturing sector diminished relative to the service sector, some unions altered their position. Organized labor continues to support foreign aid to developing countries, but would like to see it focused more narrowly on the poorest countries. Labor is worried because of the fact that the transfer of technology leads to loss of American jobs. Indeed, outflows of private capital, whether government-subsidized or not, are seen as exporting American jobs to developing countries, and technology transfers are seen as selling the "United States heritage" (Sewell and Mathieson 1982:32).

Minority and Ethnic Groups. American policies toward African and other developing countries are very much influenced by minority and ethnic groups that have more impact than their sizes might indicate. The growing interest of African Americans in United States policies toward Africa, for example, is a result of raised consciousness over civil rights within the country. In fact, there was also a growing unwillingness among African Americans to see the United States continue to support the once white-dominated regime in South Africa. This type of position made it easier for President Carter's decision in 1977 not to lift economic sanctions against

Rhodesia (now, Zimbabwe). It also forced President Reagan to implement Congress-designed economic sanctions against South Africa in the 1980s. The African American sentiment is deeply rooted in the history of the black diaspora.

As Jackson (1982:121) reminds us, there has always been a significant stratum of African Americans stimulated by the foreign policies of the United States because they have considered Africa as their original homeland. They have identified the slave labor of their ancestors as the capital which built and enriched the southern plantation economy that was fundamental to the later industrialization of the North, and which represented their investment in America's national development. It was a stake not to be surrendered at any cost. After slavery, African Americans began their entry into the foreign policy-making process in order to play a significant role in it.

Furthermore, their pursuit of power has been identified as indefatigable. From the American Colonization Society (ACS) of the nineteenth century to TransAfrica today, African Americans have continued their efforts to influence American policies toward Africa, not always in union, sometimes with contradictions, and infrequently with success. Like other Americans of foreign (though not slave) descent, African Americans have sought to use American power in the interest of their ancestral homeland. These African Americans have also looked incredulously at the ease with which immigrants born a generation ago in Europe have risen to the commanding heights of American decision making, while African Americans, rooted in America for more than three centuries, have been so systematically excluded that they have never gotten closer to the levers of executive power. This brings us to the final major question raised earlier in this chapter: What type of foreign aid doctrine did the Reagan and Bush Administrations espouse from 1980 to 1992?[3]

THE REAGAN-BUSH FOREIGN AID DOCTRINE

The Reagan-Bush victory at the polls over the Carter-Mondale ticket in 1980 revealed a shift in attitude towards the use of American power in foreign relations. Unlike the Carter-Mondale Administration which was sensitive to criticisms and ambivalence of American power overseas, the Reagan-Bush Administration took office with an articulated and internally consistent view of United States political and economic role in global affairs. This view had implications for both the international political struggle between the United States and the Soviet Union, and also for American policies in international economic matters and toward development (Eberstadt 1988:44).

According to an Overseas Development Council (ODC) Communique (1982/1), four major themes were dominant in shaping the Reagan-Bush foreign aid doctrine. These themes are (1) the meaning of power in the 1980s, (2) the nature of the Soviet Union's foreign policies, (3) the causes of the developing world's instability, and (4) the divergence and common goals of the Western alliance.

The tenet of the first theme was that an increase in American military power was necessary to reestablish American security and permit the United States to exercise its hegemony. Thus, it was perceived by the Reagan and Bush Administrations that one of the most significant challenges to American foreign policies in the 1980s was the notion that the United States had to establish a set of relations with a broad range of developing countries. It was believed that if such relations were constructive enough, United States security would be protected and enhanced.

The second theme hinged on the notion that the Soviet Union's enhanced strategic and conventional military capacities made it possible for it to become "aggressive and expansionist," thereby threatening vital American security interests. The belief here was that the Soviet Union was intent on spending as much money as possible to reach overall military superiority over the United States. Consequently, the call was made for the United States to outspend the Soviet Union if America was to put a check on that country's "aggressive and expansionist" behavior.

The presupposition behind the third theme was that the developing world was the most likely terrain for what was then referred to as the "East-West conflict" (see Hill's analysis in chapter five). Two reasons were suggested for this proposition. The first was that the developing world was an arena for increasing degree of political instability and potential regional conflicts. The second was that the Soviet Union would capitalize on such developments in the developing world to expand its (the Soviet Union's) power and influence at the expense of the West. It was, thus, believed by the Reagan and Bush Administrations that the United States should in effect attempt to raise the costs of adventurism of the Soviet Union by instituting policies that support indigenous developing world efforts to preclude Soviet intervention through whatever means they sought.

The fourth proposition emerged from the idea that the Western alliance must pay whatever price necessary to increase its military capacity in the European theater and coordinate anti-Soviet policies in the developing world. It was perceived by Reagan and Bush that there was a growing divergence between the United States and Western Europe on East-West matters and the differential results détente produced. For Western Europe, détente meant peaceful relations and rapid growth in East-West trade. For the United States, in contrast, détente produced a strong Soviet military machine that scored gains in Africa, Asia, Latin America, and the Middle East.

The foregoing premises led Reagan, especially, to embrace the foreign economic philosophies of Presidents Roosevelt and Truman, for which his (Reagan) critics were quick to label him a reactionary. Reagan emphasized this return to earlier principles during his speech in Philadelphia on international economic development in October 1981 (Eberstadt 1988:49).

During the speech, Reagan called for a reexamination of American assistance efforts to assure that they were promoting private enterprise as opposed to merely enforcing the growth of the public sector. He went on to suggest five major principles that would guide his administration's foreign aid programs. The first was that international trade had to be stimulated by opening up markets within and among countries. The second involved the proposition that development strategies had to be tailored to the specific needs and potential of individual countries and regions. The third suggested that development assistance be guided towards self-sustaining productive capacities, particularly in food and energy. The fourth called for improving the climate for private investment and the transfer of technology accompanying such investment. And the fifth was that a political atmosphere be created that would facilitate practical solutions instead of "relying on misguided policies that restrain and interfere with the international marketplace or foster inflation" (Rondinelli 1987:99).

It is no surprise, therefore, as Rondinelli (1987:100) points out, that four of these themes were reflected in USAID's Development Administration Strategy Paper issued in 1981. As he notes, USAID development administration included the following:

1. Sector-Specific Institutional Development—improving institutional performance in policy formulation, technology transfer and program management and strengthening the capacity of

institutions in high-priority sectors to provide public services and promote private investment in order to achieve "sustainable benefits for broad groups of people."

2. Strengthening Local Initiative—improving the managerial performance of local enterprises in developing countries and assisting governments to strengthen local entrepreneurship, group cooperation, local government, and provincial development "in ways that stimulate local initiative and self-help, but avoid imposing burdens on the poor."

3. Improving capacity in Management Service Institutions— strengthening the capacities of selected institutions in developing countries to provide relevant and practical management training, education, consulting, and applied research.

4. Policy Reform—supporting selectively reforms of economic, financial, and administrative policies and government structures through technical assistance and the application of new management technologies (Rondinelli 1987:100-101).

Indeed, this strategy clearly emphasized the improvement of managerial performance in developing countries' institutions, and expanding administrative capacity at the private sector. But as Eberstadt critically observers, the actions of the Reagan Administration[4] were contrary to its stated objectives. As he puts it,

> Instead of bringing America's foreign aid policies back into alignment with the goals and ideal that had originally animated them under Roosevelt and Truman, the Reagan Administration allowed American programs to continue down the path charted in the 1970s. So smooth, in fact, was the trajectory that it would be difficult to tell which administration was in power from the statements and actions of its development apparatus. No less than during the Carter years, American development programs under Reagan seemed to be at systematic variance with the objectives of the international order we nominally supported. The administrators of these programs, moreover, appeared increasingly intent upon concealing the discrepancy from the American public (Eberstadt 1988:50-51).

An empirical examination of United States foreign aid to Sub-Saharan Africa from 1980 to 1992 is needed, therefore, to determine whether the

Reagan-Bush doctrine had a positive or a negative effect on the amount of American aid that went to those countries. But whatever the results, it will be difficult to produce generalizations which can explain the philosophies of decision makers and how they interact to produce decisions. In essence, such an approach will be hampered by problems of measuring intangibles and determining values.

CONCLUSION

American foreign aid to Sub-Saharan Africa from 1980 to 1992 was geared towards reinforcing long-standing United States economic, moral, and political objectives throughout the continent because these objectives were considered to be fundamentally sound. It was a widely-held belief among American policy makers that if such objectives are sound, then, United States power in itself can be a beneficial and effective form of foreign aid.

American economic aid to Africa was used to promote development in some countries because it dovetailed with the desire to maintain existing international economic relations and at the same time to garner political influence on the continent. Aid, however, was a second-best solution for Africa: It meant neither a change in the management of United States-African relations nor a real distribution of economic benefits. In addition, because American aid was dependent on domestic and international conditions, it was an unreliable source of capital and technology for African countries.

ENDNOTES

1. On June 5, 1947, at the commencement exercise at Harvard University, Secretary of State George C. Marshall announced what came to be known as the Marshall Plan: America's interest to make significant financial contribution to rebuild a war-torn Europe. The major goal of the Plan was to promote economic integration and cooperation among European countries. Between 1948 and 1952 (when the Plan ended), $13.3 billion had been spent on the Plan, with over half of this amount going to England, France, and Italy (for details, refer to Nash 1985:42-44).

2. The Ujamaa (socialist) villages program was part and parcel of Tanzania's Arusha Declaration drawn up by Julius Nyerere in February 1967 as a means for the country to achieve self-reliance.

3. Ronald Reagan became president and George Bush his vice president after their victory over James (Jimmy) Carter and Walter Mondale in 1980. In 1984, Reagan and Bush won their reelection bid. Bush chose Danforth Quayle as his vice presidential running mate for the 1988 presidential election, which they won. In 1992, however, Bush and Quayle lost their bid for a second term to running mates, Bill Clinton and Albert Gore.

4. This is also true for the Bush-Quayle Administration, mainly because Bush was afraid of diverting from the course already set by Reagan. Some observers have cited Bush's timidity in similar matters (especially in the economic sphere) as one of the major reasons he lost the 1992 presidential election.

Chapter Five
War and Democracy in the Waning Days of the Cold War: Spillover Effects in Africa

Walter W. Hill, Jr.

INTRODUCTION

Many authors commenting on the international scene after the Second World War noted the rise in the importance of the developing countries up until the waning days of the Cold War in the 1980s. A classical, and often repeated, formulation appears in Steel (1970). He says that the international community had become characterized by four features: (1) a weakening of the Soviet bloc states; (2) a decrease in the cohesion of the Western bloc; (3) a diminished importance of nuclear weapons; (4) an increase in the number of national actors and, hence, an increase in their importance. These features are typically taken as more or less independent. I wish to argue in this chapter that the importance of the fourth issue was due to the relatively high level of conflict that was being displayed in some African countries and other areas of the developing world. I want to further argue that the conflict was at least partially driven by Steel's third point, the status of nuclear weapons in the North.

I will proceed by presenting an extended outline of the history of nuclear weapons. We will be able to recall the nearly contradictory features of an increase in the destructive capabilities of the weapons without a corresponding change in the politico-military effects. In the following section, we will see to what extent we can argue that the change in nuclear capabilities led to the United States and the Soviet Union's attempt to find other outlets for competition in a relatively safe and open arena, namely the African/Asian bloc of nations.

Historical Background

Most of Africa was colonized by western European states. The vast majority of the continent's territory was claimed in a rapid process in the late 1800s. The colonial system resulted in the African states functioning as appendages of their metropoles. Major stakes in Africa were claimed by Great Britain, France, Belgium, Germany and Italy, along with the older players of Portugal and Spain.

As a result of the Versailles Treaty following World War I, Germany's colonies in Africa were transferred to Great Britain and France. That colonial system was in place for a generation. Although France was among the winners of World War II, Paris had been occupied during the successful invasion by Germany. England had not been invaded, but the home territory suffered from attacks. One result of the war was that the economies of both France and England had been significantly weakened. The two principal remaining victorious allies, the United States and the Soviet Union, both opposed colonization. The pressure to decolonize was first successful in south Asia, with India obtaining independence in 1947. The effects were worldwide as the Gold Coast gained independence in 1957, and discarded the colonial appellation by adopting the name Ghana. The new state recalled the name of a kingdom that flourished on the Niger river. The year 1960 was referred to as "the year of Africa" because of the success of many independence movements, particularly that of Nigeria. Decolonization was to sweep across the entire continent, displacing the authority of western European political leaders.

Unfortunately, the superpowers were engaged in a Cold War and they viewed the newly independent states in only two possible categories: either the states were friends, or they were foes being allied to the adversary superpower. Political movements that had the potential to be led by nationalists were virtually required to ally with one of the superpowers. Avoiding such an alliance would result in rivals obtaining support.

By the 1980s, the much hoped for economic development of Africa, which was optimistically proclaimed around 1960, was not to be seen. Any one of a number of explanations have been proposed including the effects of the international monetary system, the weak monocrop economic legacy bestowed from colonization, the arbitrary adoption of western economic theories, and the militarization associated with the cold war.

The economies of the African states did not grow to the optimistic levels forecast at independence. The *1995 United Nations Statistical Yearbook* gives the following trade data.

Table 1. Exports from Africa to the World
and from the World to Africa (in $ billions)

Year	From Africa to World	From World to Africa	Percent
1980	3,000.9	84.4	2.8
1990	3,396.5	81.9	2.4
1992	3,686.0	82.2	2.2

Table 2. Exports from Africa to the United States
and from the United States to Africa (in $ billions)

Year	From Africa to World	From U.S. to Africa	Percent
1980	216.6	6.36	2.9
1990	374.4	6.07	1.6
1992	424.9	7.29	1.7

Note that for the United Nations, Africa includes the Mediterranean states, such as Egypt, but excludes the OPEC (Organization of Petroleum Exporting Countries) states of Algeria, Gabon and Nigeria.

By this measure, the size of the African economies actually diminished in the 1980s both in relative and absolute terms. Relative to the world economy, all of Africa constitutes between two and three percent of all trade. For the American economy, total exports to Africa also represent about two percent of trade. Despite the large geographic size of Africa, in economic terms Africa represents only a small part of the total trade.

Data on political interactions show roughly the same pattern. Consider the following pattern displayed by Azar's data. Azar counted the number of events between international actors reported in a set of newspapers. Actions with the United States as the "actor" in the period beginning 1948 also show Africa to be ignored (Azar 1980:143-152).

Table 3. Events With the United States as an Actor

Region	Number of Events	Percent
North America	4,236	14.3
South America	1,660	5.6
Western Europe	3,629	12.2
Eastern Europe	5,565	18.7
Africa	1,291	4.4
Middle East	5,333	18.0
Asia	4,088	13.8
Oceania & Others	3,905	13.1
Total	29,707	100%

The Carter Administration had an active advocate of African affairs in Andrew Young, the American representative at the United Nations. During the Reagan Administration the Soviet Union remained a prime area of concern, along with several other regions—for example, Central America. Africa typically became ignored during the Republican Administration. Perhaps the status of the region was emphasized by the elevation of Haig to the position of Secretary of State. During the Nixon Administration, Haig would pound the table with mock drumbeats whenever the subject relating to Africa was raised.

EARLY NUCLEAR STRATEGY

Let us start our overview from the end of World War II. From the American side, there was a desire among some to return to the idealized calm and prosperity of the pre-war world while somehow simultaneously avoiding another economic depression. America could perhaps return to its fortress and continue to develop. An indicated policy from this strategy is demilitarization. An alternate strategy, that of the liberal internationalists, would commit the Americans at least to involvement in Europe. With the fall of the Czech government in 1948 with Masaryk's assassination, the proclamation of the People's Republic of China in 1949, and the development of atomic weapons by America's adversaries, the main tenets of the liberal internationalist position successfully advocated American involvement in world affairs.

The most impressive part of the arsenal of both the United States and the Soviet Union was their nuclear weapons. Let us follow their development.

The dominant American strategy in the early 1950s was "massive retaliation." Under this doctrine, the United States would launch a massive nuclear attack against the Soviet Union if America were to be attacked (see, for example, Taylor 1959:23). For the strategy concerning conventional force structures, we can distinguish two periods. The first involved the extensive rebuilding of American military forces. The second was associated with the "New Look" during Eisenhower's first term (1952-1956). Note that the peak of the first phase occurred with the Korean War (1950-1952) which, in turn, was the first real case of major military conflict of the United States and the Soviet Union outside of the European theater.

By the middle of the 1950s, weaknesses in the doctrine of massive retaliation were becoming apparent. Consider Henry Kissinger who spoke of the "now obsolete weapons used over Hiroshima and Nagasaki" (1958:7). The increase in the level of terror was rapid. He stated that "nuclear weapons only a decade ago a difficult engineering feat, have now become plentiful" (1958:13-14). He observed that for all their horror, those atom bombs were "puny." He noted that the then current 20 megaton weapons were lethal at eight miles, as compared to the 1.5 mile radius of the older weapons (1958:14). Note that at this point in time, the larger weapons had become sufficiently powerful so that the prompt effects would destroy all of the inhabitants in a city the size of Washington.

Gaddis (1987:19) says that declassified archival evidence suggests that the development of "primitive" Soviet nuclear weapons "induced great caution" on American policy makers. This is consistent with the general thesis in this chapter that the United States and the Soviet Union did not want to risk a conventional war in Europe, which could escalate to a nuclear war. The costs of such a war were too great to make any projected gains worthwhile. One recalls this period with Wohlstetter's phrase, "the delicate balance of terror."

On the former Soviet side, we have Nikita Khrushchev's speech at the twentieth Party Congress in 1956. This speech is remembered primarily because of the Secretary's denunciation of Joseph Stalin. However, it should also be recalled that the speech discussed the role of the "newly independent" peoples of Asia and Africa. Of Khrushchev's three categories of wars, one was Wars of National Liberation. It is no accident that these wars were to occur far from the Soviet Union.

By the late 1950s, it was difficult to believe that the United States would respond to small challenges in a way that would lead to a massive destruction of its home territory. A doctrinal change on the American side was indicated. The change was from a policy of massive retaliation to one of flexible response. Under this doctrine, the United States was prepared to meet an attack by a response at roughly the same level of intensity. It was of course much more credible that the United States would meet a small challenge with an action at roughly the same level of intensity. A massive retaliation in response to a small challenge was not at all believable.

In other words, despite the focus of liberal internationalists on reconstruction in Europe, it was impossible for them to proceed beyond a certain level. The political system was stalemated because of the great extent to which both sides had massive arsenals of weapons. Conflict between the two shifted elsewhere. Notably to Asia, but also to Africa.

THE LATTER YEARS

The year 1960 was the "year of Africa," due to the explosion of the independence movement that took place on the continent in that year. It was also the year associated with an escalation in weaponry. The United States moved from a force structure based on bombers delivering nuclear weapons, which were opposed by air defense systems, to Inter-continental Ballistic Missiles (ICBMs), and then to ballistic missiles. These missiles cut the time from launch to impact from ten to twelve hours, to half an hour, or less. This was a clear increase in the destructive capabilities of the United States and the Soviet Union. With the advent of MIRVed (multiple independently target re-entry vehicles) weapons in the latter part of that decade, another major step was taken. Currently, in an extreme case, the top two or three officers on a Trident submarine can launch 24 missiles which carry a total of 192 warheads. There is no known effective defense against a major ballistic attack (Forsberg 1987:190).

The early 1960s were also the years of Robert McNamara. The style of conducting defense was changed. McNamara asked questions about the force structure to deter a nuclear war, minimum deterrence, the possibility of winning a nuclear war, and the value of counterforce targeting (Trewlitt 1971).

This technological sophistication supplanted the overt ideological orientation of the previous administration (Eisenhower's). We can interpret this development as being consistent with the thesis that the ideological component of the conflict between the United States and the Soviet Union had moved elsewhere.

By the end of the Vietnam War in 1973, there was an immediate problem of what new policies should be adopted. Secretary of State Edmund Muskie, part of the liberal wing of the Democratic party with respect to foreign policy issues, rejected isolationism. He identified the characteristics of American policy as (a) non-isolationist, (b) détente is an important feature, (c) while both Europe and Japan remain important, and (d) the United States must reflect on the growing interdependence between the developed and "underdeveloped" worlds. This policy, on my reading, explicitly acknowledged conflict in the developing countries and implied possible American involvement.

THE AFRICAN SIDE

As we have seen from the foregoing discussion, the destructive capabilities of the United States and the Soviet Union increased steadily from the end of the Second World War to the waning days of the Cold War. Shortly after World War II, both powers either expanded their spheres of influence or helped to install governments to their liking in Europe, broadly defined. In the orthodox literature, one typically considers one or more of the Eastern European satellites of the Soviet Union. One thereby examines the politics of Czechoslovakia and/or Hungary in the half decade after the war. By 1950, the situation was relatively stable in Europe. The only real exception was not a country, but the city of Berlin, and the outcome of the 1948 Berlin blockade foreshadowed the fact that the post-war lines were fixed.

The stability received doctrinal status. It was enshrined as the policy of "Containment." Its brother, "Rollback," faded from the scene as a policy alternative.

Outside of Europe, the situation looked different. Within Africa, American diplomatic activity in the 1950s was concentrated. Over half of the archives dealt with Congo (Kinshasa), later Zaire. The crisis involving the well-known cast of actors, Patrice Lumumba, Joseph Kasavubu, Moise Tshombe and others, weighted heavily in the United States files. One possible way of interpreting this crisis is in stark, now obsolete, East-West terms (Kalb 1983). American policy makers feared a Soviet base in Africa. Conflict between the United States and the Soviet Union at the United Nations occurred over this issue. The Kennedy Administration explicitly stated its disapproval of "another Cuba" in Africa, and it was simultaneously unwilling to confront the Soviets in Europe (say over Berlin). Note that John Kennedy was willing to militarily attack Cuba.

So, the main line of the thesis in this chapter appears to hold: American policy makers viewed the crisis in East-West terms. Yet, is there another reality? It is also possible to interpret the Congo crisis in terms of decolonization. The Congolese were placed in a position on the eve of Independence which would have made it difficult for them to have obtained true political, social and economic independence. Their leaders had for the most part had no contact with each other (some meeting in Belgium in January 1960 for the first time). They had no independent industrial base. The level of education, as measured by adult literacy rates, was low. Forced suddenly upon the world scene they desired development, but obtained little more than Cold War rhetoric. One curious footnote is that the uranium for the first atomic weapon came from Congo-Kinshasa; yet, the technology in that state was low.

Another set of cases to look at are in Southern Africa. Following a decade and half of low intensity warfare, the Portuguese government collapsed in 1974. The following year, its colonies became independent. Immediately, there was a fear in Washington that the countries of Angola and Mozambique would become proxies of Moscow (refer to Kamalu's analysis in chapter one for details on this assumption). Secretary of State Kissinger declared that Angola was strategically important, decried the communist influence in the country, and tried to get a government in Luanda more favorable to the United States. Similarly, a fear of communism was articulated in 1976 when there was a rebellion in Soweto against the policies of the Pretoria regime (see Dumbuya's discussion in chapter two for more on this).

Yet, one can easily imagine a more subtle interpretation of events. In Angola, there were several opposition movements. One supported by the United States, one by the Soviet Union, and one supported by China. This was clearly a more complex situation than would be suggested by the standard Cold War rhetoric. The groups were regionally based with different key ethnic groups involved. All were interested in economic development, and the ideological lines between them were not always clear.

Second, we can easily view the conflict in the Portuguese territories in Southern Africa in terms of decolonization and a desire for development. The South African case, though perhaps for many years explainable in East-West terms, is really a case where opposition to the former regime was fostered by the oppression of the majority of its people rather than communist instigation.

In essence, the African case appears to lend credence to the major thesis in the current chapter. Ispahani (1987:175) says it best when he suggests the following:

> ...as the United States and the Soviet Union became nuclear hostages, the vehicle for confrontation shifted from their territory and from the European theater to the Third World: To Asia, to Africa, to Central and South America.

Indeed, the African case highlights Ispahani's observation. Africa was nothing more than a pawn in the Cold War.

Conclusion

In the preceding overview, we saw that the level of nuclear technology increased rapidly in the years after World War II. This increase was so high that there was little to be gained by any military confrontation in Europe. By the early part of the Eisenhower Administration, it was clear that a battle in Europe would be disastrous for all.

A natural outlet for East-West tension was the developing countries. As we look more carefully at each of the African examples examined in the preceding section of the current chapter, we see that there were East-West tensions on the continent. Yet, one can also find an alternate interpretation of the events which centers more on issues of decolonization and development. In short order, these two alternate realities shaped the views of American actors in terms of Africa.

Bibliography

BOOKS

Adelman, I. and C. T. Taft Morris. 1973. *Economic Growth and Social Equity in Developing Countries*. Stanford: Stanford University Press.

Allison, G. T. 1974. *The Essence of Decision: Explaining the Cuban Missile Crisis*. Boston: Little, Brown and Company.

American Enterprise Institute. 1979. *Africa: US Policy at a Crossroads*. Washington, DC: AEIPR.

Baker, P. 1989. *The U.S. and South Africa: The Reagan Years*. New York: Ford Foundation, Foreign Policy Association.

Berry, J. M. 1989. *The Interest Group Society*. Glenview, IL: Scott, Foresman and Company.

Brandon, D. 1966. *American Foreign Policy*. New York: Appleton-Century Crofts.

Briggs, E. 1968. *Anatomy of Diplomacy*. New York: David McKay Company, Inc.

Carter, G. M. and P. O'Meara. eds. 1982. *International Politics in Southern Africa*. Bloomington, IN: Indiana University Press.

Chazan, N. et al. 1988. *Politics and Society in Contemporary Africa*. Boulder, CO: Lynne Rienner Publishers.

Choate, P. 1990. *Agents of Influence*. New York: Alfred A. Knopf.

Coker, C. 1966. *The United States and South Africa 1968-1965*. Durham: Duke University Press.

Danaher, K. 1986. *The Political Economy of U.S. Policy Toward South Africa*. Boulder, CO: Westview Press.

Dekin, J. 1966. *The Lobbyists*. Washington, DC: Public Affairs Press.

Dubois, W. E. B. 1967. *The World and Africa*. New York: International Publishers.

Eberstadt, N. 1988. *Foreign Aid and American Purpose*. Washington, DC: AEIPR.

El-Khawas, M. A. and Cohen, B. 1976. *The Kissinger Study of Southern Africa*.

Westport, CT: Lawrence Hill and Company.
Emerson, R. 1967. *Africa and United States Policy.* Englewood Cliffs: Prentice Hall.
Faber, M. and D. Seers. eds. 1972. *The Crisis in Planning.* Sussex: Institute of Development Studies.
Gilkes, P. 1975. *The Dying Lions: Feudalism and Modernization in Ethiopia.* London: Julien Friedman.
Hettne, B. 1978. *Current Issues in Development Theory.* Gothenburg, Sweden: SAREC Report R15.
Hrebenar, R. J. and R. K. Scott. 1968. *Interest Group Politics in America.* Englewood Cliffs: Prentice Hall.
Jackson, H. F. 1982. *From the Congo to Soweto.* New York: William Morrow and Company, Inc.
Kalb, M. 1983. *The Congo Cables.*
Kegley, C. W. and U. R. Wittkopf. 1979. *American Foreign Policy.* New York: St. Martin's Press.
Kennedy, P. 1987. *The Rise and Fall of the Great Powers.* New York: Random House, Inc.
Khapoya, V. B. 1994. *The African Experience.* Englewood Cliffs, NJ: Prentice-Hall, Inc.
Kissinger, H. A. 1957, 1958. *Nuclear Weapons and Foreign Policy.* Garden City, NY: Doubleday.
Kitchen, H. 1983. *U.S. Interests in Africa.* New York: Praeger Publishers.
Kitchen, H. and M. Clough. 1984. *The United States and South Africa: Realities and Red Herrings.* Washington, DC: Center for Startegic International Studies, Georgetown University.
Lipsen, C. B. and S. Lesher. 1977. *Vested Interest.* Garden City, NY: Doubleday and Company, Inc.
Lynch, H. R. 1978. *Black American Radicals and the Liberation of Africa: The Council of African Affairs 1937-1955.* Ithaca, NY: Cornell University Africana Studies and Research Center.
MacBean, A. I. and V. N. Balasubramanyam. 1976. *Meeting the Third World Challenge.* New York: St. Martin's Press.
Mahoney, R. D. 1983. *JFK Ordeal in Africa.* New York: Oxford University Press.
Mahood, H. R. 1990. *Interest Group Politics in America. A New Intensity.* Englewood Cliffs: Prentice Hall.
May, E. R. 1978. *"Lessons" of the Past.* New York: Oxford University Press.

Mazrui, A. A. 1977/1979. *Africa's International Relations*. Boulder, CO: Westview Press.
McKinley, E. H. 1974. *The Lure of Africa: American Interests in Tropical Africa, 1919-1939*. Indianapolis: The Bobbs-Merrill Company, Inc.
Muskie, E. S. and B. Brock. 1974. *What Price Defense?: Rational Debate Series*. Washington, DC: American Enterprise Institute.
Nielsen, W. A. 1969. *The Great Powers and Africa*. New York: Praeger Publishers.
Nisbet, R. A. 1969. *Social Change and History*. New York: Oxford University Press.
Ogene, C. F. 1983. *Interest Groups and the Shaping of Foreign Policy: Four Case Studies of United States African Policy*. Lagos: Nigerian Institute of International Affairs.
Ornstein, N. J. and Elder, S. 1978. *Interest Groups, Lobbying and Policymaking*. Washington, DC: Congressional Quarterly Press.
Parenti, M. 1969. *The Anti-Communist Impulse*. New York: St. Martin's Press.
Rondinelli, D. A. 1987. *Development Administration and US Foreign Aid Policy*. Boulder, CO: Lynne Rienner Publishers, Inc.
Rostow, W. W. 1960. *The Stages of Economic Growth: A Non-Communist Manifesto*. Cambridge: Cambridge University Press.
Samuels, M. et al. 1979. *Implications of Soviet and Cuban Activities in Africa for US Policy*. Washington, DC: CSIS, Georgetown University.
Schloming, G. C. 1987. *American Foreign Policy and the Nuclear Dilemma*. New Jersey: Prentice-Hall, Inc.
Sewell, J. W. and Mathieson, J. A. 1982. *The Ties that Bind: US Interest and Third World Development*. Washington, DC: Overseas Development Council.
Smith, H. 1988. *The Power Game: How Washington Works*. New York: Random House.
Steel, R. 1970. *Pax Americana*. New York: The Viking Press.
Taylor, M. 1959. *The Uncertain Trumpet*. New York: Harpers and Brothers Company.
Trewlitt, H. 1971. *McNamara*. New York: Harper and Row.
Turner, F. J. 1963. *The Significance of the Frontier in American History*. New York: Frederick Ungar Publishing Company.
United States Agency for International Development. 1983-1992. *Congressional Presentations*. Washington, DC: Government Printing Office.

United States Department of Commerce. August 9, 1982. *Business America*. Washington, DC: Government Printing Office.

United States Department of Commerce. June 1981. *Market Profiles for Africa* (OBR 81-41). Washington, DC: Government Printing Office.

United States Department of State. March 1982. *Development Assistance*. Washington, DC: Office of Public Communication.

United States Development Coordination Committee. 1975-1988. *Development Issues*. Washington, DC: Government Printing Office.

Volman, D. 1980. *A Continent Besieged: Foreign Military Activities in Africa Since 1975*. Washington, DC: Institute for Policy Studies.

Whitaker, J. S. 1978. *Africa and the United States: Vital Interests*. New York: New York University Press.

Wilson, G. K. 1990. *Interest Groups*. New York: Basil Blackwell.

World Bank. 1977, 1978. *World Development Report*. Washington, DC: World Bank Publications.

Woronoff, J. 1970. *Organizing African Unity*. Metuchen, NJ: The Scarecrow Press.

Zeigler, H. L. and W. G. Peak. 1972. *Interest Groups in American Politics* (2nd ed). Englewood Cliffs: Prentice Hall.

ARTICLES AND OTHER WORKS

Ajala, A. May/June 1984. Recent South African-Mozambican Negotiations. *Nigerian Forum*.

Azar, E. E. March 1980. The Conflict and Peace Data Bank (COPDAB) Project. *Journal of Conflict Resolution*. (vol. 24, no. 1:143-152).

Bishop, Jr. W. 1956. Judicial Decision. *The American Journal of International Law* (vol. 50).

Bowen, M. L. May 1990. Economic Crisis in Mozambique. *Current History*.

Chenery, H. B. and M. Bruno. 1962. Development Alternatives in an Open Economy: The Case of Israel. *Economic Journal* (pp. 79-103).

Chenery, H. B. and I. Adelman. 1966a. Foreign Aid and Economic Development: The Case of Greece. *Review of Economics and Statistics* (vol. xlviii, no. 1:1-19).

Chenery, H. B. and A. M. Strout. 1966b. Foreign Assistance and Economic Development. *American Economic Review* (vol. lvi, no. 4:679-733).

Clude, R. E. July-October 1989. The American-Soviet Confrontation in

Africa: Its Impacts on the Politics of Africa. *Journal of Asian and African Studies* (vol. xxiv, nos. 3-4).
Cohen, H. J. 1968. U.S. Measures for Peace in South Africa. *Current Policy* (no. 1218).
Crocker, C. A. September 1988. Negotiations on Angola and Namibia (Statements and Communique). *Department of State Bulletin* (vol. 88).
Crocker, C. A. November 1988. South West Africa Negotiations (Statements). *Department of State Bulletin* (vol. 88).
El-Khawas, M. A. 1984. Reagan's Policy Towards South Africa: Constructive or Destructive Engagement? *The International Journal of Politics* (vol. 1).
Entin, L. 1988. African Countries: National Security in the Making. *International Affairs* (Soviet Union). (vol. 34, no. 1:43-52).
Foltz, W. J. 1991. The Organization of African Unity and the Resolution of Africa's Conflicts. F. M. Deng and I. W. Zartman. eds. *Conflict Resolution in Africa.* Washington, DC: The Brookings Institution.
Forsberg, R. Summer 1987. Abolishing Ballistic Missiles. *International Security* (vol. 12, no. 1:190-196).
Foster-Carter, A. 1974. Neo-Marxist Approaches to Development and Underdevelopment. E. de Kadt and G. Williams. eds. *Sociology and Development.* London: Oxford University Press.
Foster-Carter, A. 1976. From Rostow to Gunder Frank: Conflicting Paradigms in the Analysis of Underdevelopment. *World Development* (vol. 4, no. 3).
Frank, A. G. 1979. The Development of Underdevelopment. K. Wilbur. ed. *The Political Economy of Development and Underdevelopment.* New York: Random House.
Gaddis, J. L. Summer 1987. *International Security* (vol. 12, no. 1:1-19).
Gambari, I. A. 1991. The Character, Fundamental Issues, and Consequences of the Conflict in the Horn of Africa. G. Nzongola-Ntalaja. ed. *Conflict in the Horn of Africa.* Atlanta: African Studies Association.
Garcia, G. D. December 26, 1988. Flowers and Drinks All Around. *Time.*
Gray, W. H. Nov. 2, 1982. Lend a Billion to South Africa? *The Washington Post.*
Griffin, K. B. and A. R. Kahn. 1978. Poverty in the Third World: Ugly Facts and Fancy Models. *World Development.*
Hodgkin, T. 1972. Some African and Third World Theories of Imperialism. R. Owen and B. Sutcliffe. eds. *Studies in the Theories of Imperialism.*

London: Longman.

Isaacman, A. May 1987. Mozambique and the Regional Conflict in Southern Africa. *Current History*.

Ispahani, M. Z. 1984. Alone Together Regional Security Arrangements in Southern Africa and the Arabian Gulf. *International Security* (vol. 8, no. 4:152-175).

Keller, E. J. 1991. The OAU and the Ogaden Dispute. F. M. Deng and I. W. Zartman. eds. *Conflict Resolution in Africa*. Washington, DC: The Brookings Institution.

Kimaru, C. M. 1990. An Analysis of U.S. Foreign Assistance to Tropical Africa in the 1980s. *Ph.D. Dissertation, University of Maryland, Baltimore Graduate School*.

Knight, R. February 16, 1987. Angola: Trapped in the Cross Fire. *U.S. News & World Report*.

Knight, V. C. May 1991. Mozambique's Search for Stability. *Current History*.

Kuehnelt-Leddihn, E. V. May 22, 1987. Namibia, Namibia. *National Review*.

Leys, C. 1977. Underdevelopment and Dependency: Critical Notes. *Journal of Contemporary Asia* (vol. 7, no. 1).

Lister, G. and M. Verbaan. January 2, 1989. Peace at Last in Namibia. *The Nation*.

Lowi, T. J. July 1964. American Business, Public Policy, Case Studies, and Political Theory. *World Politics* (vol. xvi, no. 4:677-715).

MacFarlane, S. Spring 1984. On African Security. *International Security* (vol. 8, no. 1:127).

MacLeod, S. and J. Wilde. October 17, 1988. Angola: Where Blossom and Bullets Grow. *Time*.

Maier, K. June 1989. Mozambique Offers Talks with Rebels. *The Washington Post*.

Menges, C. C. October 28, 1988. Has Anyone Seen the Reagan Doctrine? State's Angola Sellout. *National Review*.

O'Brien, P. J. 1975. A Critique of Latin American Theories of Dependency.' I. Oxaal. ed. *Beyond Sociology of Development*. London: Routledge and Kegan, Paul.

Overseas Development Council. 1982. Agenda 1982: US Foreign Policy and the Third World. *Communique* (no. :1-5).

Perkins, E. New Dimensions in U.S. Policy. *Current Policy* (no. 1253).

Reed, D. May 1987. Can This Man Save Africa. *Readers Digest*.

Reiss, S. May 2, 1988. Pulling Out of a Stalemate. *Newsweek*.

Bibliography

Sachs, R. C. 1991. Lobbying by Foreign Interests: A Japan Task Force Report. Washington, DC: Congressional Research Service Film.

Santos, T. D. May 1970. The Structure of Dependence. *American Economics Review*.

Seligman, D. December 5, 1988. Down and out in South Africa. *Fortune*.

Strobel, W. January 30, 1990. Mozambique no longer on Marxist List. *The Washington Times*.

Tarka, S. T. May/June 1984. The Message from Nkomati. *Nigerian Forum*.

TransAfrica. June 1982. Developing Africa: The Shrinking US Share. *TransAfrica Forum*. Washington, DC: TransAfrica Publications.

Valowitz, G. and R. Rolfe. September 28, 1987. An Independent Namibia? It's Still a Pipe Dream. *U.S. News & World Report*.

Wolpe, H. Winter 1988. Seizing South African Opportunities. *Foreign Policy* (vol. 73).

X. July 4, 1947. The Sources of Soviet Conduct. *Foreign Affairs* (vol. xxn, no. 4).

Younghusband, P. August 2, 1989. Mozambique Aids Easing of Tensions in South Africa. *The Washington Times*.

Index

A

Adams, John Quincy, 27
Adelman, I., 77
AFL-CIO, 47, 49
Africa Today, 58
African Americans, 53-66, 88-89
African National Congress (ANC), 16-23, 36-41
Africare, Inc., 55
AHEPA (Greek American cultural association), 50
Air Warning and Control Systems (AWACS), 45
Ajala, A., 16, 18
American Colonization Society (ACS), 89
American Committee on Africa (ACA), 58
American Conservative Union (ACU), 47
American Farm Bureau (AFB), 49
American-Israel Public Affairs Committee (AIPAC), 44-66
American Medical Association (AMA), 46, 49-50
American Negro Leadership Conference (ANLC), 61
American Telephone and Telegraph Company (AT&T), 49
Anglo-Saxon Supremacy, 82
Angola, 6-23, 34-41, 44-66, 71, 82, 102
Antarctica 31
Anti-Apartheid Act, Comprehensive, 35-41
Apartheid 3-23, 25-42, 59-66
Arab countries, 7
Arab oil boycott, 84
Arusha Declaration, 94
Arussi 7-8

Asia(n), 70, 91, 99, 103
Asmara, 22
Association of Independent States/ Confederate Russian Republics, 3-23
Atlantic slave trade, 83
Azar, E., 97

B

Balasubramanyam, V. N., 76
Bale, 7
Baker, James, 39
Baker, P., 36
Barre, Siad, 7-23
Batista, Fulgencio, 30
Belgium, 96
Benin, 69
Berbera, 8, 22
Berlin Conference, 6, 101
Berry, J. M., 46
Biafra, 61
Bishop, Jr., W., 11
Black Caucus, Congressional, 39
B'nai B'rith, 50
Borana, 7
Bork, Robert, 47-48
Botha, Pieter W., 16-23
Botha, Roelof Pik, 11
Botha, Pik W., 32-41
Botswana, 69
Brazil, 83
Brazzaville Protocol, 14-23
Briggs, E., 25
Britain, Great/British/United Kingdom, 6-23, 94, 96
Bryan, Richard H., 48
Brzezinski, Zbigniew, 10
Buell, Raymond Leslie, 54

Bulgaria, 28
Bunche, Ralph, 54
Burkina Fasso (formerly Upper Volta), 69
Burundi, 44, 69
Buthelezi, Mangosuthu, 38
Byrd Amendment, 59
Byrd, Robert C., 48

C

Cabo Delgado, 83
Cabora Dam, 18, 21
Canada, 12-23, 62
California, 65
Cameroon, 6
Cape Horn, 31, 82
Cape of Good Hope, 15, 31, 83
Cape route, 10, 30-31
Cape Verde, 69
Caribbean, 56, 62, 80, 83
Carter Doctrine, 9
Carter, Jimmy (Administration), 9-23, 31, 88-89, 94
Castro, Fidel, 13, 73
Central African Republic, 69
Central America, 03
Central Intelligence Agency, 64
Chad, 69
Chaing Kai-Shek, 30
Challenor, Herschelle, 55
Chazan, N., 74
Chenery, H. B., 78
Chile, 30
China, Peoples Republic Of, 54, 83, 85, 98, 102
Chissano, Joaquim, 19-20
Choate, P., 63
Chrome, 12, 58-59, 85
City University of New York, 54
Clinton, Bill, 94
Clude, R. E., 8, 10
Coal, 12
Cobalt, 12, 58, 85
Cohen, B., 37, 86
Cohen, Herman, 39
Cohen, H. J., 38

Cold War, 3-23, 44-67, 53-66, 95-103
Columbia Broadcasting Service (CBS), 32
Committee on Political Education (COPE), 49
Communism, 9-23, 26-42, 52, 64, 82, 102-103
Comoro Island, 83
Concerned Women for America (CWA), 47
Congo, 57-58, 60, 69, 74, 101-102
Congress on Racial Equality (CORE), 58
Congressional Research Service, 62
Connecticut, 48
Connel, Grover, 64-65
Constructive Engagement, 2, 14-23, 32-41
Containment Policy, 10-23, 32, 101
Copper, 12, 58
Cote d'Ivoire, 6
Council on African Affairs (CAA), 54-55
Council of Foreign Relations (CFR), 54-55
Crocker, Chester, 10-23, 32-41
Cronkite, Walter, 32
Cuba, 3-23, 30, 73, 83, 102
Czechoslovakia, 52, 98, 101

D

Daktari (myth), 56
Dawin's Theory of Evolution, 82
de Klerk, Frederick W., 20-21, 38-41, 60
Defense Department (US), 11
Dekin, J., 50
Dependence paradigm, 79-81
Détente, 101
Dhlakama, Alfonso, 20
Diamonds, 58
Diggs, Charles, 55
District of Columbia, 35
Djibouti, 69
Dole, Robert, 45
dos Santos, Jose Eduardo, 66
Dreier, David, 65
DuBois, W. E. B., 53
Dymally, Marryn, 65

Index

E

Eastern European bloc (former), 1, 3-23, 26-42, 101
Eberstadt, N., 91-92
Economic Commission for Latin America (ECLA), 80
Egypt, 7, 9, 82, 97
Eisenhower, Dwight D., 29, 52, 73, 99, 103
Elder, S., 50
El-Khawas, M. A., 86
Emerson, Rupert, 50, 53, 56
England/English, 52, 62, 78
Equatorial Guinea, 69
Eritrea, 23
Ethiopia(n), 3-23, 44-66, 71, 82
Europe(an), 3-23, 26-42, 52, 55, 101, 103
Executive branch, 1, 86-87

F

Faber, M., 78
Falwell, Jerry, 47
Farmer, James, 58
Fauntroy, Walter, 35
Florida, 27, 48
Foltz, W. J., 7
Foote Mineral Company, 58-59
Ford, Gerald, 75
Foreign Policy Association (FPA), 54
Forsberg, R., 100
Foster-Carter, A., 79-80
Founding Fathers, 27
Frank, Andre Gunder, 80
Free World, 26-27
French/France, 6, 12-23, 52, 94, 96

G

Gabon, 6, 97
Gaddis, J. L., 99
Gambari, I. A., 6
Gambia, The, 6, 69
Garcia, G. D., 14
Germany (formerly West Germany), 11- 23, 42, 54, 62, 83, 96
Ghana/Gold Coast, 6, 69, 96
Gilkes, P., 7
Gowon, Yakubu, 61
Graham, Bob, 46, 48
Grant, Robert, 47
Gray, W. H., 34
Greece, 42
Griffin, K. B., 78
Group Areas Act, 41
Guam, 27
Guinea, 6, 52, 69
Guinea-Bissau, 69
Gulf of Aden, 9, 22

H

Haig, Alexander, 98
Haiti, 83
Haley, Alex, 56
Harare (Zimbabwe), 8-23
Harvard Law School, 55
Harvard University, 54, 94
Hawaii, 83
Height, Dorothy, 58
Hettne, B., 75, 78-80
Hiroshima, 99
Hodgkin, T., 79
Horn of Africa, The, 2, 3-23
Howard University, 54-55
Hrebenar, R. J., 46-50
Hungary, 101
Hunton, William, Alphaeus, 54
Husein (King of Jordan), 45

I

India, 85
Indian Ocean, 9
Indigenization, 79
Inter-continental Ballistic Missiles (ICBMs) 99
Internal Revenue Code, 50
International Monetary Fund (IMF), 20
Internationalism, 27
Ireland, 54
Irish Americans, 53-54

Iron curtain, 7
Isolationism, 27, 82, 101
Ispahani, M. Z., 103
Israel, 45-66, 83
Italian American Foundation (IAF), 50
Italy(ian), 50, 54, 83, 96

J

Jackson, H. F., 54, 56, 85, 89
Jackson, Jesse, 56
Japan, 62-63
Jane (myth), 56
Jewish American, 45
Johnson, Mordecai W., 54
Johnson, Willard R., 55
Jordan, 9, 45

K

Kagnew base, 8, 22
Kahn, A. R., 78
Kalb, M., 102
Kasai, 58
Kasavubu, Joseph, 101
Katanga, 58
Kegley, C. W., 27-29
Keller, E. J., 8
Kennan, George, 29-30
Kennedy, John F. (Administration), 74, 102
Kenya/Nairobi, 3-23, 64, 69-70, 74, 82
Keynesian revolution, 76
Khapoya, V. B., 73
King, Jr., Martin Luther, 58, 61
Kissinger, Henry A., 55, 102
Kitchen, H., 52
Knight, R., 15
Knights of Columbus, 50
Korea(n), South, 62, 99
Koreagate, 64
Krushchev, Nikita, 52, 99
Kuehnelt-Laddihn, 11
Kuhn, Thomas, 80
Kuwait, 9

L

Latin America, 80-83, 91
Leahy, Patrick, 44
Lear, Norman, 47
Lesher, S., 62
Lesotho, 69
Leys, C., 78
Liberia, 69
Libya, 82
Liebermann, Joseph I., 48
Lipsen, C. B., 62
Lister, G., 13-14
Lobbying (defined), 46-47
London Conference, 56
Lowi, T. J., 58
Lukas, C. Payne, 55
Lumumba, Patrice, 101
Lynch, H. R., 55

M

MacBean, A. I., 76
MacLeod, S., 14
Mahoney, R. D., 52
Mahood, H. R., 47, 63
Maier, K., 19
Malawi, 69
Mali, 6, 69
Mandela, Nelson, 30-41
Manelik, 6
Manganese, 59
Manifest Destiny, 27, 75
Maoist ideology, 64
Maputo, 18-23
Mariam, Mengistu Haile, 7-23
Marshall, George C., 94
Marshall, Plan, 28, 42, 44, 55, 76, 94
Masaryk, 98
Mathieson, J. A., 71-74, 82-88
Mauritania, 69
Mauritius, 69
May, E. R., 71
Mazrui, A. A., 74-75
Mboya, Tom, 74
McCarthy, Joseph, 54
McCarthyism, 54

Index

McKinley, E. H., 52
McNamara, Robert, 100
Medicare, 50
Mediterranean (ea), 9, 22, 97
Mega (lobbying) firms, 63
Menges, C. C., 15
Mexico, 62
Middle East, 7, 83, 86, 91
Mondale, Walter, 89, 94
Monroe Doctrine, 27, 83
Moral Majority, 47
Morocco, 6-23, 82
Morris, C. T., 77
Moscow, 3-23, 102
Movement for the Liberation of Angola (MPLA), 12-23
Moyniham, Daniel Patrick, 48
Mozambican National Resistance Movement (RENAMO), 12-23
Mozambican Ruling Party (FRELIMO), 12-23
Mozambique, 3-23, 44-66, 71, 82
Mozambique Christian Council, 20
Multiple Independent Target Re-entry Vehicles (MIRVed), 100
Muzorewa, Bishop Abel, 56
Mzarek, Robert, 65

N

Namibia, 11-23, 39-41, 82
Nagasaki, 99
Nasser, Gamal Abdel, 82
National Abortion Rights Action League (NARAL), 47
National Association for the Advancement of Colored People (NAACP), 47, 50, 56, 58
National Association of Manufacturers (NAM), 48
National Council of Negro Women (NCNN), 58
National Education Association (NEA), 49
National Farmers Union (NFU), 49
National Organization of Women (NOW), 47
National Rights to Work Committee (NRWC), 47
National Rifle Association (NRA), 46
National Security Council (UN), 11, 16-23
National Security Study Memorandum (NSSM)-39, 33
National Union for Total Independence of Angola (UNITA), 12-23, 64
National Welfare Rights Organization (NWRO), 50
Nazi, 17
Near East, 70
Negro-American Labor Council (NALC), 58
Neto, Augustino, 12-23
Nevada, 48
New Africa, 55
New Jersey, 65
New International Economic Order (NIEO), 74, 79
New York, 15, 48, 54, 65
Nickel, 18
Niger, 68, 96
Nigeria, 6, 60-61, 82, 84-86, 97
Nisbet, R. A., 76
Nixon, Richard (Administration), 32
Nkomati Accord, 17-23, 35
North Atlantic Treaty Organization (NATO) 28, 55
Nyerere, Julius, 78, 94

O

O'Brien, P. J., 80
Ogaden, 6-23
Ogene, C. F., 57-58, 60-61
Organization of African Unity (OAU), 3-23
Organization of Petroleum Exporting, Countries (OPEC), 97
Ornstein, N. J., 50-51
Overseas Development Council (ODC), 90

P

Pacific Ocean, 83
Pan Africanism, 19
Parenti, M., 29
Park, Tongsun, 64
Party Congress (Soviet), 99
Peak, W. G., 48
Peace Corps, 75
People for the American Way (PAW), 47
Perkins, Edward, 37-38
Perot, Ross, 50-51
Persian Gulf, 9, 30
Philadelphia, 91
Pinochet, 30
Platinum, 12, 85
Poland, 54
Polish American Congress (PAC), 50
Population Registration Act, 41
Portugal/Portuguese, 6-23, 64, 96, 103
Pretoria (government), 10-23, 32-41
Puerto Rico, 27, 83

Q

Quayle, Danforth, 66, 94

R

Rabin, Yitzhak, 45
Rainbow Coalition, 56
Randolph, A. Philip, 58
Rayburn Building, 66
Red Sea, 9, 22
Reed, D., 13
Reed, Harry, 48
Reiss, S., 13
Robertson, Pat, 47
Robeson, Paul, 54
Robinson, Randall, 35, 55-66
Rolfe, R., 14
Rollins, Edward, 51
Rondinelli, D. A., 91-92
Roosevelt, Theodore, 48, 91
Rostow, W. W., 77
"Roots", 56
Rumania, 28

Rwanda, 23, 44, 69

S

Sachs, R. C., 62
Samantar, Muhammad Ali, 66
Santini Congressional Report, 85
Santos, Dos, 81
Sao Tome and Principe, 69
Saudi Arabia, 7, 9, 45
Savimbi, Jonas, 13-23, 63-64
Scandinavia, 54
Scott, 46-50
Scramble for Africa, 6
Security Council (UN), 54, 58
Seers, D., 78
Seko, Mobutu Sese, 30, 57-66, 73, 82
Seligman, 15
Senegal, 69
Sewell, J. W., 71-74, 82-88
Seychelles, 69
Shamuyarira, Nathan, 37
Sherman and Clayton (Antitrust) Acts, 48
Shultz, George Advisory Committee, 38
Sierra Leone, 6, 69
Silicon, 59
Sisulu, Albertina, 38
Sisulu, Walter, 38-39
Smith, H., 45
Sofala, 20
Somali(a), 3-23, 44-67, 69-70, 82
South Africa, 1, 3-23, 25-42, 82, 84-86, 89, 103
South African Foundation (SAF), 59-60
South African Ruling National Party, 25-52
South America, 103
South West Africa Peoples Organization (SWAPO), 10-23, 35
Southern Christian Conference (SCC), 58
Soviet Union, 3-23, 45-66, 83, 95-103
Soweto, 39
Spain, 96
Special Drawing Rights (SDR), 84
Stalin, Joseph, 99
State Department, 10-23

Index

Steele, R., 95
Strobel, 21
Sudan, The, 44, 69, 82
Suez Canal, 82
Swaziland, 69
Sweden, 83
Swiss bank accounts, 64
Switzerland, 83

T

Taiwan, 30
Tambo, Oliver, 38
Tanzania, 69, 78, 94
Tarka, S. T., 17
Tarzan (myth), 56
Taylor, M., 99
Texas, 50
Thomas, Clarence, 48
Tin, 58
Togo, 69
Torricelli, Robert, 65
Toure, Sekou, 52
TransAfrica, 35, 55-66, 70
TransAfrica Forum, 61
TransAfrica News, 61
Trewlitt, H., 100
Trident submarine, 100
Truman Doctrine, 28
Truman, Harry S., 28, 30, 42, 47, 91
Truman Plan, 28
Tshombe, Moise, 101
Turkey, 42
Turner, F. J., 72

U

Uganda, 69
Ujaama, 78, 94
Union Carbide Corporation, 58-59
Union for Total Independence Of Angola, (UNITA), 12-23
United Democratic Front (UDF), 38
United States Agency for International Development (USAID), 69-92
United States Chamber of Commerce (USCC), 48
United States Export-Import Bank (USEB), 21
United Nations Organization (UNO or UN for short), 10-23, 54, 58, 97-98
Uranium, 12

V

Valowitz, G., 14
Vanadium, 85
Vance, Cyrus, 10
Verbaan, M., 13-14
Vermont, 44
Versailles Treaty, 96
Vietnam, 28, 83, 101
Volman, D., 83

W

Walters, Ronald, 55
Wars of National Liberation 99
Washington Office on Africa, 59
Washington, George, 27
Washington, Robert B., 66
West Virginia, 48
Western Europe, 9-23
Western Five (Contact Group), 12-23
Western Sahara, 6-23
Western Somalia Liberation Front, 7-23
Whitaker, J. S., 53
White House, 11, 38, 51
Wilde, J., 14
Wilkins, Roy A., 58
Wittkopf, U. R., 27-29
Wolpe, H., 15
World War I/II, 11-23, 26-42, 48-66, 95-103
Woronoff, J., 9

X

"X" pseudonym, 29

Y

"Year of Africa", 100
Yergen, Max, 54
YMCA, 54

Young, Andrew, 55
Younghusband, P., 20

Z

Zaire, 30, 57-66, 69-70, 73, 82
Zambia, 12-23, 69
Zeigler, H. L., 48
Zimbabwe (formerly Rhodesia), 12-23, 37-41, 55-58, 69, 89

Contributors

ABDUL KARIM BANGURA holds a Ph.D. in Political Science from Howard University, a Ph.D. in Policy Sciences (concentration in Development Economics) from the University of Maryland Baltimore Graduate School, and a Ph.D. in Linguistics from Georgetown University. He is Researcher-In-Residence at The Center for Global Peace and Assistant Professor of International Relations in the School of International Service at American University, and Director of The African Institution.

MOHAMED SULAIMAN DUMBUYA is a doctoral degree candidate in Political Science at Howard University. He also is affiliated with the United States Department of Transportation.

WALTER W. HILL, JR. received his Ph.D. in Political Science from the Massachusetts Institute of Technology. He is Associate Professor of Political Science at St. Mary's College.

NGOZI CALEB KAMALU received his Ph.D. in Political Science from Howard University. He is Professor of Political Science at Fayetteville State University, Fayetteville, North Carolina.

CHRIS M. KIMARU holds a Ph.D. in Policy Sciences (concentration in Economics) from the University of Maryland Baltimore Graduate School. He is Assistant Professor of Public Administration at North Carolina Central University.

SOCIETY AND POLITICS IN AFRICA

Yakubu Saaka, General Editor

This multidisciplinary series publishes monographs and edited volumes that provide innovative approaches to the study and appreciation of contemporary African society. Although we focus mainly on subjects in the social sciences, we will consider manuscripts in the humanities that treat context as a significant aspect of discourse. Within the social sciences, we are looking for not only analytically outstanding studies but, what is more important, ones that may also have significant implications for the formulation and implementation of public policy in Africa. We are especially interested in works that challenge pre-existing hierarchies and paradigms.

For additional information about this series or for the submission of manuscripts, please contact:

> Peter Lang Publishing
> Acquisitions Department
> 275 7th Avenue, 28th floor
> New York, New York 10001

To order other books in this series, please contact our Customer Service Department:

> 800-770-LANG (within the U.S.)
> (212) 647-7706 (outside the U.S.)
> (212) 647-7707 FAX

Or browse online by series at:

> www.peterlangusa.com